D1036413

Informed Consent

A Primer for Clinical Practice

Informed Consent

A Primer for Clinical Practice

Deborah Bowman
Professor of Bioethics, Clinical Ethics and Medical Law, Centre for Medical and Healthcare Education, Division of Population Health Sciences and Education, St George's, University of London, UK

John Spicer
Director of GP Education and Head of School, London Commissioner for Medical and Dental Education, University of London, UK

Rehana Iqbal
Consultant Anaesthetist and Lecturer in Medical Ethics and Law, St George's Healthcare NHS Trust and Centre for Medical and Healthcare Education, Division of Population Health Sciences and Education, St George's, University of London, UK

CAMBRIDGE
UNIVERSITY PRESS

CAMBRIDGE UNIVERSITY PRESS
Cambridge, New York, Melbourne, Madrid, Cape Town,
Singapore, São Paulo, Delhi, Tokyo, Mexico City

Cambridge University Press
The Edinburgh Building, Cambridge CB2 8RU, UK

Published in the United States of America by Cambridge University Press, New York

www.cambridge.org
Information on this title: www.cambridge.org/9781107688063

First published 2012

Printed in the United Kingdom at the University Press, Cambridge

A catalogue record for this publication is available from the British Library

Library of Congress Cataloguing in Publication data
Bowman, Deborah.
Informed consent : a primer for clinical practice / Deborah Bowman, John Spicer, Rehana Iqbal.
    p. ; cm.
Includes index.
ISBN 978-1-107-68806-3 (pbk.)
1. Informed consent (Medical law)   2. Physician and patient.   I. Spicer, John, 1954–   II. Iqbal,
Rehana.   III. Title.
[DNLM: 1. Informed Consent – ethics.   2. Mental Competency.   3. Physician-Patient
Relations. W 85]
R724.B645   2011
610–dc23
                                                                                        2011025062

ISBN 978-1-107-68806-3 Paperback

Contents

Chapter

1

Introduction to clinical consent: laying out the territory

Introducing consent

The process of seeking the consent of a patient to a medical procedure is, arguably, one of the most important skills a doctor, or indeed any clinician, should learn. In fact, the very idea that doctors may institute diagnostic or treatment processes of any sort without a patient's consent is utterly counter-intuitive to the modern practice of medicine.[1]

It was not always thus, and even now it can be reliably assumed that consent is still not sought and gained appropriately in every clinical encounter. To say that it should be sought and gained in this manner elevates the value of consent to a high level. It can be instructive to ask oneself why such a value might be held to be the case. The answer to this question lies in the philosophical underpinning of clinical consent, which sits within a notion of personal autonomy, and respect for autonomous decision-making. When we say that autonomous decision-making should be respected, we are endowing individuals with the ability to make their own decisions about their individual futures.[2] It is a philosophical axiom that this should be so, with a long history attached.[3]

Within that history, the best reference point is probably the Enlightenment: that flowering of science, arts and philosophy in the eighteenth century. Admittedly the Enlightenment was a primarily European phenomenon, but, notwithstanding that, it could be said that the dominant theme emerging from the Enlightenment was actually that of personal autonomy and the right of individuals to make decisions about their own futures.[4]

As such, it may have built on even older traditions from the Ancient World, and was certainly related to emerging political changes in the New World, but the notion that individuals (and indeed collections of individuals) could behave in this way and have rights so to do was indeed new. Previously, it should be noted, individuals in Europe lacked access to such rights, being confined within religious, monarchical or other structures. So medical consent as it is interpreted today stands not in clinical isolation but on a history of political change.

To this, we must add a more recent tendency in Western medical practice to be specific, personalized and clear about consent. Despite the Enlightenment ideals of centuries ago, it would be true to say that the practical application of

Fig. 1. A representation of doctors' duties.

autonomous reasoning by patients lacked a certain substance, at least until the later part of the twentieth century. Why might this be so?

To answer the question, it is necessary to consider medical decision-making more thoroughly. Consider the diagram in Fig. 1 as a representation of doctors' duties: they can be conceptualized in three ways as overlapping areas of interest.

Doctors will always need to practice within a framework of law, given by the country, or jurisdiction, within which they work. In the UK, this framework is determined by statute law, common law and a host of quasi-legal government orders. In a sense, the legal environment is a compulsory version of the ethical mores that pervade the same country. Ethics, of course, is more complex than that: any given country will generally contain a variety of peoples following differing ethical codes. These ethical codes spring from many sources: religious, secular and personal, all and each of which systematize the answers to the rather simple questions: 'What is the right thing to do?' or 'What is the right sort of person to be?' The impact of this kind of diversity on medical practice, including that pertaining to consent, is fairly clear: clinicians need to develop an understanding of the values important to all their patients, reaching accommodations with their own values, within the prevailing legal environment in order to practice ethically sound medicine. Whatever those values are, shared or personal, they drive individuals' decisions about their lives and are thus intimately linked to autonomous choice. Respect for autonomy is one of the four key medical ethical principles described and articulated by Thomas Beauchamp and James Childress, two American philosophers who have had enormous influence on clinicians' understanding of ethics.[5] There will be few health professionals currently working who have not heard of beneficence, non-maleficence, justice and respect for autonomy. Whilst the strength of this 'principlist' analysis is undoubted, although often contested, other moral perspectives will be considered in succeeding chapters.

The third element of Fig. 1 is professionalism. Doctors need also to remember the professional duties associated with their practice, and in the case of the

UK, these are determined by bodies including the General Medical Council (GMC). This regulatory authority interprets the law and sets standards to which doctors must adhere in order to practise in the UK. Other healthcare professionals have their own governance bodies setting similar standards of practice. For nurses in the UK, it is the Nursing and Midwifery Council who fulfil this function. Professional bodies do not necessarily share the same constitutional arrangements, intra-professional make-up or procedures, but the principles of professional guidance are common.

So, in broad terms, clinicians considering the area of consent will need to remember the law pertaining to consent, the professional rules surrounding consent, and the ethical basis of consent and autonomous reasoning. These will be amplified in succeeding chapters, and we will focus on the general issues surrounding consent with particular reference to its relevance in day-to-day clinical practice. For this reason, the text is liberally sprinkled with case examples and their analysis. Professional and ethical approaches tend to dominate, and where legal frameworks are discussed, they will have a UK bias, although comparative reference is occasionally made to other jurisdictions. Clinical problems are still manifestations of patient suffering, wherever they may occur around the world, and this is the starting point for this book. Simple guidance as to 'what to do' or 'what to say' in seeking and gaining a person's consent to a medical intervention is dealt with in many procedural guides,[6] signposted throughout the text, but we also hope to open out the theoretical substructure of consent and its clinical application for the reader to reflect upon.

Challenges for the clinician

Ethical dilemmas are often cast in terms of possible actions and outcomes. Consider the following:

> Andy Milton presents to the accident and emergency department of a rural hospital, with superficial injuries, sustained in a fight in the street outside a public house. He is intoxicated, and therefore a full account of the episode is difficult to determine. While treatment for his injuries is being given by Dr Berry, the emergency medicine registrar, a police unit arrives in the department and the officers make enquiries as to whether anyone has arrived after a fight at the local pub. Andy is made aware of the presence of the police by the clinical staff, but he requests – and indeed requires – them not to tell the police of his presence or medical state. Dr Berry considers what she should do.

This clinical encounter is easy to conceptualize as one of consent: Andy Milton is not consenting to the release of any information about his state to law enforcement officers, so the dilemma for the duty registrar appears clear: should she cooperate with Andy's instruction? There are legal issues that are relevant, for example the various statutes on police enquiries[7] and the common law on medical confidentiality.[8] The registrar will also be aware of GMC guidance on sharing clinical information with agencies such as the police.[9] Dr Berry will also consider what would be the morally right thing to do, and there are various perspectives available to her. It could be argued that she should decide which approach is liable to generate the best consequences, and this may include how she might foster the prevention of further street disturbances, or treatment of any possible alcohol misuse by the patient. She may regard Andy's view as absolutely determinative, as a rule she cannot ignore and to which he has an inviolable right. All of these ethical perspectives focus on the action: whether Dr Berry should be guided by Andy's refusal or not.

Perhaps less familiar, but no less rigorous, is consideration of the scenario from the point of view of Dr Berry herself. What moral qualities might it be relevant for her to show in dealing with this case? Analysing cases from this point of view illustrates the *virtues* necessary for the practice of medicine. We could say that she should display courage (if she has to refuse the police request or even Andy's), integrity (in holding to the moral decisions she might make) and wisdom (in fully considering her position and discussing it with colleagues). This sort of ethical analysis is both ancient and modern – it forms the basis of the Hippocratic Oath – and consideration of what it means to be a virtuous practitioner is a re-emerging feature of medical ethics discourse today.[10] These three separate ways of considering the ethical aspects of the situation reflect the three most important strands of moral theory described. To give them their more usual descriptors: theories concerned with the moral value of outcomes and consequences are *consequentialist* or *utilitarian*, those concerned with duties and rights are *deontological*, and those concerned with the moral agency of the people involved are *virtue* theories.

Clinical consent: its composition

Most authorities recognize four components to valid medical consent, as follows:

- Adequate information.
- A capacitous (competent) patient.
- Freedom from coercive influence.
- Dynamism: the continuing nature of consent and the ability to withdraw permission.

These components form the chapter headings for this book, dealing with each in sequence. Thus, any consent sought and gained by a clinician of a patient should have all of these elements fully addressed to be professionally, lawfully and ethically sound. It is a high standard to reach, and thus could be held to merit the attention it is given in this text and elsewhere. A term often heard in daily clinical practice, and seen in the literature, is the shorthand 'informed consent'. This form of words has a particular legal meaning in the US, which will be described in Chapter 3. In the UK, the use of 'informed consent' does not imply primacy of the information component over the remaining three listed above. Valid consent requires consideration of all four components.

It should also be noted that, whereas there is an enormous amount of literature that describes and analyses the components of consent to do with information provision and capacity, there is relatively little published material about the exercise of free and dynamic consent. Among other aims, this book attempts to correct that imbalance and to give due consideration to these two underdescribed areas.

Forms of consent

For now, we shall first consider forms of consent, in which all of these components are considered, in various degrees, to be involved. A US case from 1914 offered what is still a fine statement of law summarizing medical consent. Justice Cardozo said: '*Every human being of adult years and sound mind has a right to determine what shall be done with his own body* …'[11] He was making an ethical statement about capacity and status, and founding it on a rights analysis (more common in the USA than the UK in 1914). Judge Cardozo then put a sting in the legal tail by going on to say '*… and a surgeon who performs an operation without his patient's consent commits an assault, for which he is liable in damages.*'

Even allowing for the intervening hundred years or so, this short summary of law is still relevant. Doctors who operate or initiate any medical intervention without consent can face legal consequences and may have to pay damages or endure other consequences such as disciplinary action. So, to update to the early twenty-first century, consider the following judicial quotation:

Recognizing an individual right of autonomy makes self-creation possible. It allows each of us to be responsible for shaping our lives according to our own coherent or incoherent – but, in any case, distinctive – personality. It allows us to lead our lives rather than be led along them …

This is actually a secondary quotation by Lord Steyn, a judge in a UK medical negligence case.[12] The original quote is from one of the finest pieces of medical ethics writing ever seen.[13] His Lordship too conjoins ethics and law in his judgment, and uses this form of words to amplify his opinion that '*due respect is given to the autonomy and dignity of each patient*', and in doing so, is agreeing with Judge Cardozo, from earlier times, the primacy of the patient's consent to medical intervention. Both these examples are deliberately chosen both to illustrate the close relationship between law and ethics and also the enduring nature of the principles that lie behind the law. Consent and autonomy mattered as much at the start of the twentieth century as at the start of the twenty-first.

However not all medical interventions are surgical operations and the question should be asked as to how patients and doctors should define and implement the seeking and obtaining of consent. Various forms are in use and will be summarized below.

Express consent is sought from patients when it is thought to be necessary. This rather vague form of words captures its vague application. All surgical procedures, minor or major, need an express form of consent, where at the conclusion of discussion between doctor and patient, written forms are signed to evidence the acceptance of the procedure. In recent years, these forms have become more detailed and complex.[14] Some authors have even suggested pre-printing consent forms with all complications listed by procedure.[15] The value of standardized forms is in the prompts to professionals to discuss the relevant material with patients. However, it should be remembered that these forms are merely types of evidence that a discussion has taken place between doctor and patient, not that full understanding has been achieved, or legal immunity acquired, or indeed anything else.

Implied consent is just that: the assumption by a healthcare professional that the patient permits the intervention without the full legal panoply of a consent form, or even necessarily a discussion about the process. This is probably much more common in the day-to-day practice of clinical medicine, where the formal seeking of consent is not done, abbreviated or recorded. Consider the scenario below.

> Bhupinder Singh attends his primary care clinic to discuss some foot stiffness he has been having over the previous few months. Dr Whinny examines the relevant joints and then writes out some forms for blood tests, asking him to go to another part of the clinic to have the tests done. He does suggest some differential diagnoses to Bhupinder and asks him to return. He also offers to check Bhupinder's blood pressure, as it has not been taken for a couple of years. He happily rolls up his sleeve to accommodate the sphygmomanometer cuff.

Implied consent was probably operating in at least three ways in this consultation. When the patient unlaced his shoe, took off his sock and presented the offending foot to the doctor, we could say that he was, in effect, consenting to the visual, and probably tactile, examination. Indeed, his presence in the clinic that day with those symptoms could be taken to be indicative of some measure of consensual engagement.

Considerably more invasive than a foot examination is a blood test and the phlebotomist may have checked that Bhupinder was happy to proceed as he sat in the relevant chair. The story does not record whether he knew what blood tests he was destined for, or the ramifications thereof. Finally, Bhupinder seemed cheerful about having a blood pressure check, where the doctor proceeded again on the presentation of the arm. There are issues in each of these encounters to do with how much information he might have had, or whether he was coerced into these actions, and these will be dealt with in later chapters. The point to note here is that consent was not written, expressly given or acknowledged as such – given the limitations of the scenario. It may be perfectly legal, though arguably less moral, and certainly not adequately professional.[16]

There are various other categories of medical consent described in texts and guides: tacit consent, verbal and written consent, explicit and implicit consent, and others. It is our suggestion that none contains as clear a distinction as that between express and implied, and should preferably be set aside.

The context of medical consent

It is a truism that conversations between clinicians and patients about consent, choice and decision-making do not take place 'in a box' insulated from the ward, clinic or the wider milieu.[17] A traditional view would be that a relationship of trust exists between doctor and patient, where the former has only the latter's best interests at heart; and therefore the seeking and gaining of consent to medical intervention is merely a formality. This approach clearly does not capture the subtlety of the interaction. Other factors that mediate the nature of the discussion include the clinical judgement of the clinician,[18] the skills and the seniority of the clinician and some practical considerations such as time available for discussion.[19]

Of particular interest in the developed world currently is the issue of availability. A perfect notion of autonomous choice that a patient might exercise could include all possible types of available intervention. Consider the case below.

Gregorius Pawlicki, aged 50, is discussing options for control of his morbid obesity with his physician, Dr Wellington. He has a body mass index of 45 and several co-morbidities. Both doctor and patient agree that weight reduction is going to be an important part of his care. They review options, which include dietary intervention, exercise regimes, appetite-modifying drugs and bariatric surgery. On balance, and after much thought, Gregorius prefers a surgical approach. His clinician agrees but then has to pass on to the patient the news that recent budget cuts will prevent him accessing this intervention. Gregorius is not pleased and threatens to involve local politicians.

On the face of it, a well-conducted evaluation of options has led to a dissatisfied patient. Although full formalized consent to bariatric surgery has not yet occurred, Gregorius has made an autonomous choice, supported by a full discussion with his advisor. The rehearsal of management options is now held to be a vital part of patient decision-making, and one way in which the trust relationship is realized.[20] To have concealed the surgical option may have led to a less difficult conversation but is hardly consistent with the manifestation of trust. In any event, information about alternatives in treatment is more generally available than it was, for various practical and social reasons. This can be conceived as social progression, the sharing of professional power or even as part of a consumerist change.[21]

Thus, resource constraints can also affect the potential for decision-making, choice and, ultimately, clinical consent. The larger issue that needs confronting in this sort of case is beyond clinical consent, in its barest form, and touches on the duty of the doctor to reveal all the possible interventions that might be available: essentially a duty of truth-telling or of candour. As such, this area reflects the scope of information transfer and will be dealt with in Chapter 4.

Conclusion

We have seen thus far the ways in which consent can be described as a formalization of respect for the ethical principle of patient autonomy. Successive chapters will explore the components of that principle, as described in the first box in this chapter. In essence, the aim of these theoretical approaches is to maximize the choices available to persons under clinical care, maximizing respect for autonomy in the process. Although such choice can be limited by factors outside clinical control[22] (e.g. economic, organizational and social factors), the duty nonetheless remains with the clinician not to indulge in a paternalist constraint of choice

This theme, as hinted at the top of this chapter, that medical practice has moved to a less paternalist mode in recent years is consistent with other approaches to modern ethical practice described in the relevant literature. Under this heading would be found the issues of patient-centredness,[23] narrative-based care, shared decision-making (between doctor and patient)[24] and the notion of therapeutic alliance.

A greater attention to the theory and practice of good clinical consent therefore does not stand on its own but reflects more general trends in the humanization of medical practice in recent years.

As stated, this book now opens up into detailed consideration of the four components of valid clinical consent: its implicit aim is to provoke reflection, as well as to inform. One way of doing that is simply to read and think. We suggest that the reflective process may be better stimulated by putting the book aside after each clinical case scenario and conjuring up thoughts and ideas, before moving on to the next section. We suspect that the overall aim of rendering assistance to the healthcare practitioner may be better made in this way.

Resources for further reading and amplification of points made are to be found in the notes. They are for enthusiasts only, and should not necessarily be seen as 'compulsory'.

Endnotes

1. See Manson, N. C. (2010). Consent and informed consent. In R. Ashcroft, A. Dawson, H. Draper and J. McMillan, eds., *Principles of Health Care Ethics*, 2nd edn, pp. 297–304. Chichester: Wiley; O'Neill, O. (2003). Some limits on informed consent. *J Med Ethics* **29**, 4–7; Meisel A. and Kuczewski, M. (1996). Legal and ethical myths about informed consent. *Arch Intern Med* **156**, 2521–6.

2. Delany, C. (2008). Making a difference: incorporating theories of autonomy into models of informed consent. *J Med Ethics* **34**, e3.

3. See O'Neill, O. (2002). Autonomy, individuality and consent. In *Autonomy and Trust in Bioethics*, pp. 28–48. Cambridge: Cambridge University Press.

4. Isaiah Berlin's famous essay, *Two Concepts of Liberty*, in *The Proper Study of Mankind: an Anthology of Essays* (1997), H. Hardy and R. Hausher, eds., London: Chatto and Windus, is a key analysis of the political and social aspects of Enlightenment thinking.

5. Beauchamp, T. and Childress, J. (2001). *Principles of Biomedical Ethics*, 5th edn. Oxford: Oxford University Press.

6. Not least of which is the *Reference Guide to Consent for Medical Examination or Treatment*, 2nd edn (2009). London: Department of Health. Available at http://www.dh.gov.uk/prod_consum_dh/groups/dh_digitalassets/documents/digitalasset/dh_103653.pdf.

7. In England and Wales, police enquiries are governed for the most part by the Police and Criminal Evidence Act 1984, as amended.

8. *W v. Egdell* [1990] 1 All ER 835 is the leading case on medical confidentiality. There are a variety of UK statutes relevant to specific areas of clinical practice.

9. General Medical Council (2009). *Confidentiality*. London: General Medical Council (paragraphs 53–55).

10. For a brief overview of virtue theory, see Rachels, J. (1995). Feminism and the ethics of care. In *The Elements of Moral Philosophy*, pp. 160–172. Singapore: McGraw-Hill. See also Toon, P. (2002). The sovereignty of virtue. *Br J Gen Pract* **52**, 694–5; and Toon, P. (2002). Defining and cultivating the virtues. *Br J Gen Pract* **52**, 782–3.

11. *Schloendorff v. Society of New York Hospital* [1914] 211 NY 125.

12. *Chester v. Afshar* [2002] EWCA Civ 724; [2003] QB 356.

13. Dworkin, R. (1995). *Life's Dominion: an Argument about Abortion, Euthanasia and Individual Freedom*. London: Harper Collins.

14. See http://www.dh.gov.uk/prod_consum_dh/groups/dh_digitalassets/@dh/@en/ documents/digitalasset/dh_4074657.rtf for a standardized UK written consent form.

15. Rahman, L., Clamp, J. and Hutchinson, J. (2011). Is consent for hip fracture surgery for older people adequate? The case for pre-printed consent forms. *J Med Ethics* **37**, 187–9.

16. Getz, L., Sigurdsson, J. A. and Hetlevik, H. (2003). Is opportunistic disease prevention in the consultation ethically justifiable? *BMJ* **327**, 498–500.

17. Corrigan, O. (2003). Empty ethics: the problem with informed consent. *Sociol Health Illn* **25**, 768–92.

18. Judgement can be argued to be similar to the ancient attribute of *phronesis*, or practical wisdom. See Downie, R. S. and Macnaughton, J. (2000). *Clinical Judgement: Evidence in Practice.* Oxford: Oxford University Press.

19. Powerfully argued in Tallis, R. (2009). *Hippocratic Oaths.* London: Grove Atlantic.

20. Elwyn, G. (2008). Patient consent: decision or assumption. *BMJ* **336**, 1259–60; Parks, J. A. (1998). A contextualised approach to patient autonomy within the therapeutic relationship. *J Med Humanities* **19**, 299–310.

21. Slowther, A., Ford, S. and Schofield, T. (2004) Ethics of evidence based medicine in the primary care setting. *J Med Ethics* **30**, 151–5.

22. Agledahl, K. M., Forde, R. and Wifstad, A. (2011). Choice is not the issue: the misrepresentation of health care in bioethical discourse. *J Med Ethics* **37**, 212–15.

23. See Launer, J. (2002). *Narrative-Based Primary Care: a Practical Guide.* Oxford: Radcliffe Press.

24. Marshall, M. and Bibby, J. (2011). Supporting patients to make the best decisions. *BMJ* **342**, 775–6; Gulland, A. (2011). Welcome to the century of the patient. *BMJ* **342**, 792–5.

Chapter 2

On capacity: can the patient decide?

Introduction

This chapter will deal with that element of clinical consent termed, most commonly, capacity. The philosophical underpinnings of the term will be considered, along with the practical implications of evaluating a person's capacity. The law relating to capacity varies around the world, and reference will be made to differing judicial approaches and interpretations.

What, then, is capacity in a clinical context? In fact, it is difficult to separate a general view of clinical capacity from that in other areas: it is simply a person's ability to consider something and to make a decision about it. In the domain of consent, it is held to be the ability to give consent or to refuse treatment. In other chapters, we consider issues that are substantively different: whether consent is coerced or uninformed for example. Each of these elements of consent assumes that the person of whom consent is sought is able to understand the nature and implications of the decision.

Clearly, many clinical problems will undermine, or at least influence, a person's ability to consent to an intervention. Young children, those with age-related cognitive impairment or patients suffering toxic confusional states may all have impaired ability to give consent. Although it is important to stress at the outset that capacity is not automatically considered to be impaired by virtue solely of a particular diagnosis, the emphasis is on function and not pathology. When capacity is thus impaired, then it follows that others – perhaps relatives or clinicians – could give consent on behalf of a thus-impaired patient. These latter agents we can call proxies, as they act on behalf of an impaired person. When and where this can be justified, legally or morally, we will consider later.

Clarification is called for as to meaning: under the heading of informed consent, the words 'capacity' and 'competence' may be used interchangeably.[1] Challenging as that may be to semioticians, it is easier for clinicians to work with, and is advised if only because of the ways in which the relevant laws have evolved using both terms. UK law generally refers to minors as being 'Gillick competent' if they have attained a level of understanding conferring the ability to consent lawfully. The features underlying Gillick competence should be considered in a similar fashion to those underlying capacity in the cognitively impaired patient.

What is understanding?

When we say that someone has the ability to consent or to refuse treatment, we are suggesting that the cognitive function of a person is at a level that supports that assertion. There are some other criteria that could be applied as well: that the person's understanding is not limited by illness, immaturity or irrationality, for example.

Consider the following scenario.

> Dorothea Simmond has recently recovered, for the most part, from a left-sided stroke. She is cared for in a rehabilitation ward and has made considerable progress in overcoming her initial weakness and speech impairment. She does have limitations to her thinking, getting rather confused when discussing medical aspects of her treatment. Previously, her health was fairly good, suffering only hypertension, which was well controlled despite the stroke thereafter. Prior to her admission, she had lived alone since becoming widowed 10 years ago.
>
> She is being considered for discharge, and a particular local residential home seems to suit her needs. The clinical team discusses this aspect of her care with her, but she resolutely wishes to return home. They are concerned that she may not cope at home, and consider her capacity to make this decision.

An analysis of Mrs Simmond's understanding of her situation might be helpful here, and the obvious question to be considered is 'understands what?' This is important: understanding as a notion is inevitably linked to the fact of the matter needing to be understood. So we might explore with her what she knows about her upcoming discharge, how it will affect her and other related issues. Clinicians are used to applying tests of cognition, such as the Mini Mental State Examination.[2] These are not tests of decisional understanding or, more formally, legal assessments of capacity, as they do not assess a person's judgement or reasoning.[3] Both of the latter assessments are considered in more depth below. Contrast the level of understanding that may be needed between a decision that Mrs Simmond may make to allow nursing staff on the ward to perform a simple procedure such as changing a dressing with that needed to facilitate a discharge to her home where physical and social needs are inevitably greater. Ultimately, the capacity being defined in these sorts of areas is that necessary to support a particular decision and the gravity of the decision demands a particular level of understanding. Therefore, in this example, the team might explore with her the following areas:

- The extent to which her medical problems might influence and affect decisions about her discharge to live in her existing home.
- The available and alternative residential options.
- Mrs Simmond's perceptions of returning home including her priorities and wishes.
- The possible risks (physical and social) of Mrs Simmond's return to her home and her appreciation of those risks.

This list is not intended to be exhaustive but has been given simply to demonstrate that such assessments are examining aspects of mental functioning that are beyond simple cognition. There are standardized tests of mental capacity available, and the reader is directed to sources where full accounts are described.[4] It could be inferred that the most important aspects of determining the degree of decisional understanding are those referable to the outcome of the scenario or, more precisely, the range of potential outcomes. Ultimately, a decision is a form of action directed towards a particular consequence, of many possible consequences, and the cognitions and psychological processes that support that action are, arguably, the most important ones of all. Interestingly, a judge in a UK consent case argued this point too, conferring legal standing to this philosophical position.[5]

Discussion of the philosophical complexities of causation is beyond the scope of this book, but it may be useful to step back a moment and consider something of the ethical basis of intellectual capacity. Thus far, we have argued that a respect for autonomous decision-making is a *sine qua non* in clinical practice. As such, this may no longer be held to be contentious, but by extension we could say that decisions that are not capacitous, or that reflect some diminished intellectual function below a certain point, may not be worthy of such a respect. Such a modified position would need a strong ethical justification: essentially these kinds of situations where incapacitous decisions are essentially overruled or ignored are termed paternalist.[6] Moral agency implies a capability to reason, which is, as far as is known, an exclusively human phenomenon and is linked to any descriptive version of incapacity we might describe. For Dorothea Simmond, her decision-making around her discharge or indeed any other aspect of her clinical care or aftercare implies a capability to reason her way through her situation and the alternatives she is confronting. Tests of mental capacity already mentioned are merely an operationalized way of assessing those skills.

Moving from ethics to law, in England and Wales, there is now a statute governing issues of mental capacity – the Mental Capacity Act 2005[7] – and this supplants the prior common law.

This Act is a complex piece of law with many new provisions, although its five key principles can be summarized as follows:[8]

1. Capacity in adults is presumed.
2. A right to supported decision-making.
3. A right to make eccentric or unwise decisions.
4. Centrality of best interests.
5. Finding the least restrictive alternative of those available.

This then is the legal and ethical backdrop to Mrs Simmond's discharge decision: a valid decision should be informed, free and capacitous, and to have legal force that capacity should be consistent with the principles outlined above.

Clinicians dealing with her case should therefore reflect on whether the care and conversations they have with her about the discharge are similarly consistent. It will be evident that a level of capacity, that is, the capability to understand, reason and decide, is going to differ with the nature of the decision. When and where to leave hospital after a serious illness are markedly different decisions from choosing between, for example, coffee and tea in mid-afternoon, and thus demand a 'higher' level of understanding and thinking. As will be seen later in this chapter, the nature of capacity assessments does confer a certain power to the clinician simply by virtue of these various levels of seriousness.

It will also be noted that any capacity assessment that supports Mrs Simmond in her decision to return home confers on her a certain responsibility as well. It follows that she accepts responsibility for her actions from any informed, capacitous and free decision so to do.[9] This is not quite as straightforward as it might appear. Should the clinical team examine her capacity, find it adequate for her decision and then arrange discharge home with an appropriate package of care, it is insufficient to argue that she has taken full responsibility for a situation about which both they (and she) may have qualms. This is an issue of some importance to the clinician, who may be in the business of assessing risk for vulnerable patients at home. Whilst it may be logical to accord full responsibility for the assumption of risk to a capacitous patient in a situation such as that of Mrs Simmond, most clinicians would still wish, within a continuing professional relationship, to keep a watchful eye on her progress over time. This might necessarily include a review of her physical and mental state in context, with additional interventions as needed, even if capacity is maintained. These aspects will be explored further in Chapter 4 on voluntariness. A related, if dissimilar, problem is encountered in the borders between clinical capacity and criminal responsibility, the latter being the concern of specialist forensic psychiatrists, rather than of all clinicians.[10]

There is a footnote to this kind of case that merits explanation and applies to UK decisions that are concerned with housing and the incapacitous. Since the passage of the Mental Capacity Act 2005, and its implementation over the succeeding years, any decision by a clinical team involving housing changes for incapacitous patients may need the involvement of other professionals. Where the incapacitous patient does not have a family member to advocate for them, an Independent Mental Capacity Advocate (IMCA) must be instructed to assist. This legal duty also extends to the provision of serious medical treatment where neither relatives nor a properly appointed proxy are to be found.[11]

Let us now turn to some of the other issues that we have suggested above as having the potential to undermine a patient's capacity: immaturity, illness and irrationality.

Immaturity: the younger patient

In any analysis of capacity, it is convenient to divide children into two groups. Quite clearly the infant or toddler is in no position to make important decisions about their future in the manner described above. Certainly toddlers may make decisions about which toy to select and play with, or whether to demand food, drink or a cuddle at any particular time. As such, this can be seen as a developing sense of autonomous function, to be encouraged and assisted by caregivers. However, clearly there is a gulf between such decisions and those affecting medical care and the like. Nonetheless, the power of children to understand such decision-making grows as they mature. As such, this notion of growth neatly matches that which defines the only clear difference between children and adults: children grow, and adults, biologically, do not.

Clinicians need to have ways of assessing understanding in the same way, or at least to the same end, as is done in the cognitively impaired person represented above. The aim here is to define when a child is able to give an informed consent to medical procedures. Traditionally, this has been done chronologically and Table 1 summarizes the lawful age of consent to various other behaviours in various jurisdictions.

Clearly, there are differences between countries, founded on the social mores behind the laws. If anything, the table illustrates the difficulties of defining the maturation of minors chronologically. Furthermore, such a way

Table 1. Lawful age of consent

Issue	Age of consent (years)	Country	Notes
Drinking alcohol	21	USA	Can vary between states
	None	France	18 to buy alcohol
	18	UK	5, in private, with parents
Sexual intercourse	15	France, Poland	
	16	UK	
	18	Malta	
Driving	17	UK	18 for cars with trailers
	16	USA	Most states
Marriage	18	UK	16 with parental consent
	21 (male)	India	18 for females
	18	USA	Most states, usually 16 with parental consent

of controlling, or attempting to control, a minor's behaviour does not help very much in rationalizing the role of understanding in consent for medical processes. The rather paternalistic legal rules described above are generalized to whole populations, rather than being based on an individual's capacities, and rest on a notion of the best interests of the minors concerned, as well as the wider social implications involved. In clinical practice, a more individualized standard is necessary, and would be intrinsically more ethical if so. Certainly, the best interests of the minor are a key component of a capacity decision, and this aspect returns this analysis to the interrelation of the two issues.

It can be helpful here to differentiate two aspects of paediatric care: there is the legally driven notion of capacity (or competence) as one part of a formal informed consent process. Where the minor has achieved a level of understanding defining capacity, and other elements are satisfied, then we say informed consent can be taken from the child.

Good paediatric care can also be described in a less formal but nonetheless relevant notion of *assent*. To engender trust in the doctor–patient relationship and to assist a developing capacity, it has been suggested that assent should be sought in dealing with children's care. This is a relatively recent strand in the literature of care.[12] What is described here is how seeking a child's assent to treatment may involve, for example, telling the patient what is to be expected, helping them understand the medical process in an age-appropriate manner and considering willingness to accept care. This notion of assent may even stretch to allow children to defer or even refuse a medical intervention. Historically, children had little connection with their medical care in this way, being done to rather than done with, on the explicit consent of parents or guardians. Moreover, as a child matures chronologically and therefore intellectually, the possibility of engaging in formative assent conversations similarly develops, and with this the possibility of fostering trust relationships between the clinician and the minor.

As stated above, this would still be the case with the incapacitous child: those who are very young or older children with persistent intellectual handicap. Medical consent necessarily must be taken from a proxy offering *substituted judgement* of the case. It is assumed that this proxy acts in the *best interests of the child* in question. Let us divert briefly to a discussion of what that might mean.

Children, capacity and best interests

UK law recognizes the term *welfare* more precisely than the term *best interests*, although for most purposes clinicians can regard them as interchangeable in this context.

In supporting a child's welfare, the following factors are described in the UK Children Act 1989[13] as being illustrative:

- The ascertainable wishes and feelings of the child concerned.
- Physical, emotional and educational needs.
- The likely effect on him or her of any change in his or her circumstances.
- His or her age, sex, background.
- Any harm which he or she has suffered or is at risk of suffering.

This area is not always straightforward. In most clinical contexts, it is easy to determine, using the principles of the Children Act 1989, what is in the best interests of a minor, and in older minors, the patients themselves have a voice in its determination.

However, in the very young, very ill minor it may not be so easy. The UK courts have seen a succession of such cases over the last 20 years where parents and medical teams have differed markedly in how the concept of 'best interests' and welfare are interpreted. Many of these cases concern decisions at the start of life in premature infants. Clearly, such babies cannot exhibit capacity in any sense of the word. Thus, proxies – parents, courts or clinicians – make decisions on their behalf. Strictly, clinicians do not actually make decisions for such infants but simply act in their best interests in the absence of consent. All these proxies follow the same conception of best interests, or at least should do. Occasionally, a clinician's view may not coincide with a parental view and it is useful to develop a notion of best interests in more detail for these patients.

Ruhal Priti is born at 23 weeks' gestation after a complicated pregnancy. She showed no spontaneous respiration at birth and required total support in a specialized neonatal intensive care facility (NICU). Over the next 2 weeks, it became evident that she was significantly neurologically compromised as a result of her prematurity. The NICU team assessed her prognosis as poor, with a short expectation of life. Her subjective distress was difficult to evaluate. After lengthy discussions with her parents, Ruhal's cardiovascular support was removed at 3 weeks and she died.

These sorts of cases are irredeemably sad, medically complex and ethically demanding. From the point of view of medical consent, several issues seem pertinent. As an incapacitous patient, Ruhal has to rely on others to make proxy decisions for her, including those concerning the final life-sustaining treatments and their withdrawal. Usually, the people who act as proxies for young children are the parents working with the clinical team. In this example, her parents will have been informed by the clinical team as to the prognosis, awareness and other issues in her care. Ruhal's connection to the world around her, as described by her awareness, is of key importance here. It is self-evidently a physiological factor, based on the maturity of her nervous system at 23 weeks' gestation, but it is also an ethical issue, as it is part of the attribution of moral value to fetuses as they develop. This is a complex area, where ethical positions lie between those who would argue that we should attribute the same value to embryos as full-term newborns and those who would only attribute the same value to those born with (approaching) a full capacity to interact with others.[14]

Lawfully, the team must make a decision about withdrawal of treatment in her best interests, in the terms described above. We might reasonably assume that Ruhal was suffering by virtue of her multiple interventions in the NICU (despite the best intentions of the team) and was perhaps destined to suffer more as a result of her premature birth and its sequelae. In this way, an ethical justification for the removal of life-sustaining treatment is made, and this is legally supported in most of the cases that have come before UK courts.[15] Problems can arise when the parental view of such patients' best interests and the medical view do not coincide. How then should such key decisions be taken for these incapacitous infants? Whilst it may be argued that parents should have primacy over clinicians in deciding these matters, principally because they are biological proxies who will have the most caring to do for Ruhal should she survive into childhood, the cases that have come before courts in the UK have generally applied the best interest principle throughout. For the most part, this judgement uses suffering, prognosis and distress as the most relevant elements. Medical evidence as to these factors is always heard and weighed in the balance by the courts, and this is clearly particular to the case in hand: all courses of action have their relative merits and demerits. Where parents insist on invasive treatment in the absence of evidence that it will alleviate suffering, then courts will generally find against them and allow withdrawal of treatment.[16] This is not a general rule and on occasion courts have agreed with parents' preferences for invasive treatment where circumstances have suggested to the judges that the best interests of the child dictated that.[17]

The developing child's capacity

It is a truism that the only difference between paediatric and adult clinical practice lies in the fact of a child's growth. Although perhaps an oversimplification, it is useful to apply the growth principle to the acquisition of capacity as a child ages. Between the clearly incapacitous toddler and the mature adult, a minor will develop physically and mentally, and in doing so will acquire the potential to make a capacitous decision. It will depend on the nature of the decision under consideration, and may even temporarily regress. Given the variation between children, this threshold will occur at differing chronological ages, and will depend also on the context of the family and environment.

Consider the following case.

Yvonne Brown is a vivacious and bubbly 10-year-old girl. She has two older brothers of 13 and 17 years. She has been troubled by plantar warts for the previous few years. Her parents have applied salicylic acid creams every night, with which Yvonne has cooperated, although not always gracefully. They are spreading quite rapidly across the sole and further treatment options are considered.

One afternoon, Yvonne attends her local clinic with her mother, having been booked in for liquid nitrogen treatment by a dermatologist. This turns out to be rather painful, and Yvonne protests, withdrawing her leg from the reach of the doctor. After a great deal of discussion, they decide to abandon the treatment and try again another day.

On the next occasion, Yvonne has come round to the idea of cryotherapy and has decided to 'be brave'. After two treatments, her warts resolve.

If Yvonne was 18 years old, we would accord her full rights to decide about her treatment as she thinks fit. Why might we hesitate with Yvonne's decision at this stage?

One objection could be based on her understanding of the implications of the natural history of plantar warts and the role of cryotherapy, such that she may not be able to analyse rationally the harms and benefits thereof.

Harms may include complications of the procedure itself, long-term problems with pain and infections, against the benefits of a (probable) cure. If Yvonne could consider all these things, and others, then it is difficult to resist the notion that she has a measure of overall understanding and thus may consent or refuse her cryotherapy. Ten-year-old children are clearly on the borderline of understanding, and that understanding is going to vary among individuals. On the face of it, a decision about cryotherapy is not a particularly serious medical intervention: warts are not life-threatening, although they can and do interfere with many activities valuable to children, and we may posit a rather lower standard of understanding necessary in Yvonne to consent to treatment compared with that necessary for a surgical procedure involving anaesthesia. Nonetheless, much depends on the interactions between Yvonne, her parents and the clinical staff. Where the aim is to foster trust between Yvonne and her doctors, and respect her thinking and decisions, then a more ethical series of conversations must take place, whatever the outcome for her warts.

For the arguably more pressing issues in consent for medical processes, although the principles are similar, a legal view may assist. For many years in the UK, there was no clear settled law on the consent of 'borderline' minors such as Yvonne. Where a minor achieved the chronological age of 16, then medical consent was always given and capacity was assumed. The Family Law Reform Act 1969[18] allowed minors of 16 and 17 years to consent to medical procedures as if they were at the age of majority (18 years), but the situation of capacitous minors under 16 years was not addressed. Incapacity was assumed, and parents or guardians took proxy decisions on medical issues for their children.

It took the case of *Gillick v. West Norfolk and Wisbech AHA*[19] to bring about some clarity (limited by further developments) to working with this age group. In summary, the UK Law Lords brought about a common law justification for according legality to medical decision-making in minors who could demonstrate a version of understanding of the decision in question. *Gillick* was a case concerning access to contraceptive advice and treatment, but it applies to the whole of medical decision-making.

What has become known as *Gillick* competence (and inappropriately as Fraser competence)[20] is actually a capacity standard. Arguably, it is a higher standard than any standard described up to this point, and much academic critique has flowered on this observation.[21]

English law has a built-in catch to contend with. Several years after *Gillick*, a couple of other cases came before the Court of Appeal[22] that distinguished a refusal of treatment from consent to treatment. The full reasoning is beyond the scope of this book, and both cases concerned vulnerable teenagers with mental health problems, but in summary the settled law is as follows. Even if a minor is *Gillick* competent, then a refusal of medical treatment can be overruled by a parent or a court as long as that treatment is held to be in the minor's best interests. Further cases since have upheld, for example, the lawfulness of requiring a Jehovah's Witness minor to submit to blood transfusion during treatment for leukaemia, among others.[23] The passage of the Mental Capacity Act 2005, whose principles have already been described, has slightly clarified this complex area of law and medicine for 16- and 17-year-old persons. Under this provision, young people in that age group who suffer impaired mental functioning, and are incapacitous therefrom, as a result of a brain disorder are treated as if they were 18. Where they are not so afflicted, then the (confused) common law applies.[24]

It is difficult to mount a philosophical justification for distinguishing refusal and consent to medical treatment and we do not attempt to do so here. In practical terms, circumnavigation of this element of the common law is achieved in the UK, consistent with the notion of assent as described above. In these rarely reported cases, *Gillick*-competent minors with chronic and life-limiting diseases have been involved in refusals of further treatment, where patient, parents and medical teams are all in agreement. One such, reported only in the lay press, involved a 13-year-old girl who faced a lifesaving heart transplant as her only means of survival. She, her parents and her doctors all agreed that this was a step too far, given a long and complex medical history. At one point, a case was raised in law by the local primary care trust to oblige her to undergo the transplant, which the patient and her family resisted. Ultimately, the case was dropped, the young girl survived longer without surgery than she was expected to do, and some time later she changed her mind.[25]

These issues can be contrasted usefully with those where the interaction of clinical law and practice conjoin in relation to sexual health advice and care. In Table 1, it was noted that the age of consent to sexual intercourse varies in differing jurisdictions. Clearly, teenagers may not, and do not in the UK, despite its illegality, wait for the attainment of 16 years before becoming sexually active. As we have seen, the *Gillick* case concerned the way in which healthcare professionals can lawfully offer sexual health advice and treatment to those minors who may come their way. Real life is even more complicated than that of course, and some minors may become sexually active even before the UK legal limit of 13 years, below which no lawful consent to sex can be given.[26] Strictly speaking, as this is so, clinicians must refer any such cases they come across to the police: thus, anyone having penetrative sex with a minor under the age of 13 years is guilty of assault or rape.

Clinicians working in the arena of sexual healthcare will therefore encounter some difficult cases to work with. Even if a minor is *Gillick* competent to consent to the medical services surrounding sexual activity, he or she may not, under statute, consent to sexual intercourse under the age of 13 years, and this activity is in any event illegal below the age of 16 years.

They will also need to be aware of the possibility of sexual abuse occurring at any time below the age of 18 years. Statute law is clear for this under-13 age group, and by implication any clinicians encountering such minors who are having penetrative sex should involve the police or child protection authorities.[27] There may be a dilemma, however, in that clinicians may feel this is not necessarily in the best interests of the minors involved, and would wish to exercise discretion about such a referral. In the 13–15-years age group, sexual activity may be consensual, even if unlawful. In the *Gillick* case referred to above, the judges all considered whether a doctor's provision of contraceptive advice could be held to be facilitating this unlawful activity. The tension therefore in all these situations is between a child's capacity to consent to sexual intercourse and the way the law regards the nature of the act. Clinicians are advised in these difficult circumstances to be aware of the relevant statutes and professional guidelines, and to act accordingly. Departure, in clinical practice, from these sources of guidance would be a rare event, only undertaken with senior and supported advice.[28]

Illness and capacity

Illness, as we have already seen, can affect capacity, and therefore the ability to consent meaningfully: this is clearly the case for both children and adults. For adults, however, it is an issue coloured by the fact of demographic change and the relative increase in proportions of older, and vulnerable, people. These are the clinical situations where consideration of capacity and consent is most salient.

Dorothea Simmond, the example above, has cerebrovascular disease and it seems to be affecting her capacity. In itself, that is unsurprising: any disease that may undermine central neurological function and the reasoning and cognitive skills that flow from it is likely to affect capacity. These processes can affect all age groups, but it is particularly the case with illnesses that are progressive, such as dementia or Huntington's disease. We therefore need to consider issues of capacity in relation to the older patient in more detail, taking into account the three approaches to clinical duties described in the introductory chapter.

Some illnesses can affect capacity temporarily, and therefore capacity can fluctuate. Consider the case below.

> Zena Surma is an 80-year-old woman who lives with her daughter and son-in-law. She is normally quite well, looking after herself in a 'granny flat' adjoining the family home. Her daughter called the general practitioner (GP), Dr Patel, to see her as she was becoming confused and complaining of abdominal pain and frequency of urination. A urine test was positive for nitrites, leukocytes and protein. Dr Patel suggested treatment with an antibiotic, being mindful of a prior history of recurrent urinary tract infections.
>
> He spoke to Zena about her illness and the suggested treatment but found that she could not understand much of the information he was trying to get across. He decided to assess her capacity for the decision about her antibiotic treatment.

This rather commonplace story illustrates several things. Firstly, it seems that Dr Patel was assuming that Mrs Surma had capacity, until her mental state suggested that it might not be so. Secondly, her usual state did not give rise to the observation that she might be incapacitous. Only in response to the (presumed) urinary tract infection was the possibility of incapacity raised. This is not surprising: it is known that acute illnesses can interfere with cognition, cause confusion and undermine a patient's understanding and reasoning. Thirdly, it leaves the GP in a quandary as to who could or should give consent for Zena's evidently necessary acute treatment.[29] To address these issues, we need to consider the legal framework governing informed consent in this sort of clinical scenario. Let us first finish the story of Zena, by way of introduction.[30]

> Dr Patel formally assessed Zena's capacity and found her to be incapacitous for the treatment decision. He discussed her care with her relatives and identified the use of an antibiotic to be in her best interests.
>
> Thus, without Zena's fully informed consent, he arranged for her family to administer the course of treatment.
>
> As he drove back to the primary care centre, he hoped he had helped to reduce her incapacity by so doing.

So apart from the clinical decision-making, what kind of assessment of capacity should Dr Patel apply to Zena, where his concern has been raised that she may, at that time, and for that decision, be incapacitous? Earlier in this chapter, we considered what an analysis of understanding may include: the Mental Capacity Act 2005, building on the principles described earlier, offers us the legal meaning of capacity as a formalized set of steps as follows:

Can the person:

1. Understand the information relevant to the [medical] decision?
2. Retain the information?
3. Use or weigh up information as part of decision-making?
4. Communicate the decision (by any means)?

If the patient can do all these things, then he or she is legally capacitous. We can assume that Zena could not demonstrate these things for Dr Patel, at the time of the discussion, and for that decision.[31]

It should be noted that this four-limbed structure is not specific to medical decision-making: it is general. It should also be noted that legal capacity is a more specified notion than what has been described thus far. It has a practical flavour that cannot but be of help to the healthcare professional in day-to-day care. The reader is directed to several sources that amplify application and interpretation of the Act in these terms. By way of summary, a capacity assessment process to determine the ability to consent in a medical context could be illustrated as shown in Fig. 2.

The notion of a best-interests decision merits some further detail. Thus far, we have discussed the meaning in relation to children, and mainly from the legal point of view. In general terms, working in the best interests of patients is a professional duty, and it would be difficult to conceive of clinical practice without that overall aim. In a discussion about consent, a best-interests decision is made as an alternative to a capacitous decision by a patient and as such is a fairly momentous action by a doctor, who should think carefully as to what that might involve.

Firstly, an ethical duty would include consideration of doing some good for the incapacitous person, and doing no harm (beneficence and non-maleficence, respectively). For Zena Surma in the case above, any treatment option should capture those principles. We have seen how treatment of her urinary tract infection might actually augment her ability to reason, think and understand – even rendering her capacitous for other decisions – and is thus beneficent. In elderly persons, the choice of antibiotic can be capable of good or, quite easily, harm, given the potential of some antibiotics to cause serious untoward effects.

Secondly, even though relatives in this situation may have no legal ability to consent for her treatment, they will have knowledge of what Zena may have wanted if she was capacitous. As her main carers, they will probably also have

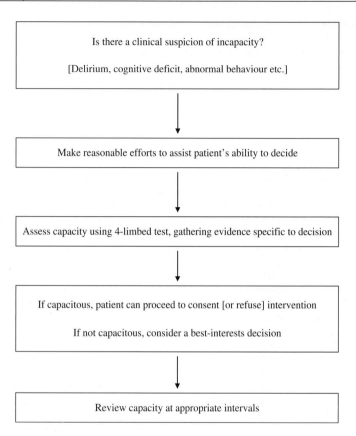

Fig. 2. Capacity assessment.

an awareness of her day-to-day life: her likes and dislikes, her needs and wants, her preferences and choices. Any of this may be relevant to decisions about her treatment taken in her best interests.

Thirdly, even though Zena was found to be incapacitous for the decision about antibiotic treatment, this does not exclude her participation in other aspects of her care to the maximum of her ability. In practical terms, this might include, for example, the encouragement of oral fluid intake or other measures relevant to the clinical situation.

Table 2. Best interests and the Mental Capacity Act 2005

Make no assumptions about the patient
Consult others who know the patient
Encourage participation of the patient in their care
Take the least restrictive alternative
Caution with life-sustaining decisions

The Children Act 1989 has helpfully fleshed out what the term best interests might mean for young people, and the Mental Capacity Act has done the same for adults with incapacity. Clinicians, and indeed any other professionals dealing with incapacitous patients, are encouraged to consider the summary in Table 2; further detail is available from documents already quoted.

Several other aspects of incapacity law as it stands in the UK now bear further comment. The Mental Capacity Act 2005 formalized the role of Independent Mental Capacity Advocates. These are relatively new professionals who support and represent those without capacity in various ways, including in relation to medical and social care.[32] They must be involved where there is no other support for the incapacitous person, when serious medical treatment is proposed or an accommodation change may occur. They may be involved similarly in adult protection processes or care reviews.

Changes have also been brought about under the 2005 Act to powers of attorney providing for Lasting Power of Attorney (LPA), which may be either financial or personal welfare in type. The latter type is a new phenomenon in the UK as it allows persons to draw up an LPA giving medical decision-making powers to relatives or other 'qualifying persons'. These are drawn up by a person when capacitous, looking forward to a time when they are not. There are limitations on the donee with respect to life-sustaining treatments. This proxy decision-making is both new to the UK and rather similar to the proxy decision-making of parents for incapacitous children in principle.[33]

Other jurisdictions around the world have had such substituted-judgement processes for many years. Quebec, for example, empowers 'surrogates', who are usually the next of kin, to make medical decisions for incapacitous patients as part of its Civil Code. Other Canadian provinces have similar provisions.

The salient ethical point concerning substituted judgement for incapacitous patients' decisions is this: it should reflect what the patient would have wanted had he or she not been incapacitous. In this way, autonomous choices are preserved through the period of incapacity. Canadian surrogates, or UK donees, are not deciding what they themselves would want as a medical outcome but what the incapacitous patient would want. Clearly, on occasions this is going to be difficult to determine and may involve consultation with others, but nonetheless the principle applies.[34]

Irrationality and eccentricity

As stated above, the Mental Capacity Act 2005 does not proscribe decision-making of an eccentric nature. Clinicians need to be aware of this provision because patients often make decisions that seem odd, unaccountable or unreasoned. It can be a source of anxiety for clinicians when patients decline, for example, treatment that might be life-sustaining, life-giving or otherwise in their best interests.[35]

That the law upholds this approach is founded on the ethical basis of autonomous decision-making. For those who can reason, are relevantly informed and free, the best judge of an individual's best interests is self-evidently the individual themselves. Even if this opinion is not shared by a clinician, it is difficult to justify a paternalist approach and overrule a person's decision. If nothing else, eccentricity is a relative notion among people.

> Qurra Hussain is afraid of needles and always has been. He finds, in middle life, that he has acquired a serious allergy to bee stings. He consults Dr Boyle, an allergist, who recommends that he carries a supply of adrenaline (epinephrine) for subcutaneous injection should he get stung by a bee. This advice is given as Qurra has suffered an anaphylactic reaction in the last month or two. Qurra declines this suggestion despite the allergist's strong recommendation. They agree to differ.

It might seem irrational that Mr Hussain has allowed his dislike of needles to overwhelm what may be life-saving medical advice. It may be that we can describe his preferences as a needle phobia, given sufficient associated emotional symptomatology, although that is missing the point. There may even be personal psychopathology attached to his dislike of needles. Severe fears and phobias are not usually rational, although the more severe the phobia, the more understandable the reaction.

It is likely that the allergist is thinking of Qurra's best interests in formulating his advice, but that conception of best interests is pretty narrow, taking in his best medical interests. This more or less approximates to his survival in the face of a possible life-threatening anaphylaxis: it is essentially a utilitarian point of view, taking in the consequences of a clinical decision as much as anything else. Of greater value is the nature of Qurra's decision-making as a capacitous and independent person. He dislikes needles, as most of us do, but in this case that dislike escalates to the stage of potential for real harm: that is part of the personal value system he espouses. It is worthy of respect in itself as a demonstration of autonomous decision-making.

Some challenges

Thus far, the discussion has centred on decisional status: how a person's capacity, or lack of it, has affected clinical consent and refusal. Thus, we have mainly been considering issues of cognition and neurological functioning leading to rational or otherwise decisions. There is something lacking in this framework, depending as it does on formalized capacity assessment. A broader view of the incapacitous patient might take account of several other themes.

Incapacitous patients may be so temporarily or permanently, depending on the pathology or perspective causing the incapacity. It is difficult sometimes for clinicians caring for patients with an episode of illness and incapacity to be aware of, or even know, the life course of that patient. In other words, how decisions the patient might make, or might have made, fit into his or her life goals and values. This may be easier for primary care clinicians who do, generally, have longer-term relationships with patients and their families.

Revisiting the case of Zena Surma above, and her urinary tract infection, the story ended with the GP reflecting on one of the reasons for his course of action. We open the case up again here to consider one last aspect. Where patients are temporarily of limited capacity, by definition their potential for autonomous reasoning is also necessarily limited. One of the recurring themes of this book is that respect for the principle of autonomy is of pre-eminent importance as an ethical value. Thus, anything the clinician can do to bring about a patient being more autonomous than he or she was before such an intervention is also of immense ethical value. In the case of Zena, treatment for her urinary tract infection can do just that, by abbreviating her confusion and reducing her incapacity. One author has termed this *fostering autonomy* and defined it as a key medical duty.[36]

Conclusion

In this chapter, the reader has encountered the major issues surrounding the capacity element of clinical consent. We have chosen to begin with issues of capacity because it is the gateway to an ethically complete consent. Where patients may not be capacitous, then further consideration of, for example, information understanding or transfer is rendered most difficult, if not impossible. Incapacitous patients, almost by definition, are among the most vulnerable people liable to be encountered by clinicians and perhaps have the greatest moral claim on their services.

It remains only to clarify who among healthcare teams should be determining whether a patient has capacity in the terms described. Our contention is that all medical students and doctors, whether working in primary or secondary care, should develop and maintain the assessment of capacity in their skill set, as it is a core clinical skill. The demands of clinical practice and changing demography would suggest that this skill is going to be needed more and more over the coming years, and thus should not be relegated to those (e.g. psychiatrists, geriatricians and general practitioners) who may consider capacity more than most. Certainly, there will be a role for consultation between doctors in borderline or complex cases, and that is clearly only good practice anyway. Medical professionals do not have a monopoly on this area of practice, and many other social and healthcare professionals also require knowledge and skills in capacity assessment.

The demography bears further comment. The pattern of relatively large numbers of patients with long-term, age-related cognitive decline is going to accelerate over the coming years, at least in Western societies, and will have enormous implications for healthcare providers. They will have to ramp up care, facilities and professional skills in dealing with this group of complex patients. Whilst a full review of the ethics of dementia[37] is beyond the scope of this chapter, it could be said that healthcare professionals might usefully consider it as a developmental aim beyond understanding consent and capacity in the terms that they have been described here.

Our illustrative examples in this chapter have been patients suffering from strokes, prematurity, skin disorders, needle phobia and urinary tract infections. All of them have been described briefly, limiting descriptions of their wider contexts to that practical in the text, but in reality, the value of that wider context will be vital in any consideration of the impact of incapacity. The principles we have described can be generalized to all patients who are, or might be, incapacitous. This includes a vast array of patient presentations: consider the intoxicated patient staggering through an emergency department, the frightened woman in labour, the non-concordant teenage diabetic, the drug-dependent socially disadvantaged prisoner and so many other similar clinical scenarios.

The issues articulated in this chapter will apply to all of them, and it is hoped the discussion and resources identified will assist practitioners in thinking their way through seeking and obtaining consent for their necessary management.

Endnotes

1. Bielby, P. (2005). The conflation of competence and capacity in English medical law: a philosophical critique. *Med Health Care Philos* **8**, 357–69.

2. Versions of this test abound: see http://www.pennine-gp-training.co.uk/Mini-Mental-State-Exam.doc for a useful example.

3. Raymont, V. (2002). 'Not in perfect mind': the complexity of clinical capacity assessment. *Psychiatr Bull* **26**, 201–4.

4. Letts, P. (ed.) (2011). *Assessment of Mental Capacity: a Practical Guide for Doctors and Lawyers*, 3rd edn. London: British Medical Association and Law Society.

5. Per Lady Butler Sloss in *Re: MB [Medical Treatment]* [1997] 2 FLR 426.

6. Joel Feinberg has referred to the overruling of incapacitous decisions as *weakly* paternalist (where the overruling of capacitous decisions is strongly paternalist). See Brock, D. (1998). Paternalism and autonomy. *Ethics* **98**, 560–5.

7. The Scottish equivalent, enacted some years before, is the Adults with Incapacity [Scotland] Act 2000. Northern Ireland has no statute, only common law, although a Bill will be introduced in 2011 following an official review.

8. See the British Medical Association publication at http://www.bma.org.uk/images/ mentalcapacityactguidanceaug2009_tcm41-190120.pdf.

9. See Glannon, W. (2002). *The Mental Basis of Responsibility*. Burlington: Ashgate.

10. Meynen, G. (2009). Exploring the similarities and differences between medical assessments of competence and criminal responsibility. *Med Health Care Philos* **12**, 443–51.

11. *Mental Capacity Act 2007: Code of Practice* (2007). London: HMSO.

12. Committee on Bioethics (1995). *Informed consent, parental permission, and assent in pediatric practice. Pediatrics* **95**, 314–17. Available at http://www.cirp.org/library/ ethics/AAP/. See also Alderson, P. and Montgomery, J. (2001). *Health Care Choices: Making Decisions with Children*. London: IPPR.

13. Part 1, s. 1(3).

14. For a full account of this issue, see Ford, N. (2007). The moral significance of the human foetus. In R. Ashcroft, A. Dawson, H. Draper and J. McMillan, eds., *Principles of Health Care Ethics*, 2nd edn, pp. 387–392. Chichester: Wiley.

15. Rennie, J. M. and Leigh, B. (2008). The legal framework for end-of-life decisions in the UK. *Semin Fetal Neonatal Med* **13**, 296–300.

16. *Re: OT* [2009] EWHC 633 [Fam]. For a full discussion of withdrawal of treatment in the incapacitous infant, see General Medical Council (2010). *Treatment and Care towards the End of Life: Good Practice in Decision-making*. London: General Medical Council. Available at: http://www.gmc-uk.org/End_of_life.pdf_32486688.pdf; and BMA British Medical Association (2007). *Withholding and Withdrawing Life-prolonging Medical Treatment: Guidance for Decision-making*, 3rd edn. London: British Medical Association.

17. *Glass v. United Kingdom* [2004] (application no. 61827/00).

18. Section 8(1).

19. *Gillick v. West Norfolk and Wisbech AHA* [1986] AC 112, [1985] 3 All ER 402, [1985] 2 BMLR 11 [HL].

20. English law references the parties to the case in citations, and not the judges hearing the case. Hence, *Gillick* as shorthand for the emerging principle from the case cited above. See Wheeler, R. (2006). Gillick or Fraser? A plea for consistency over competence in children. *BMJ* **332**, 807.

21. Alderson, P. (2007). Competent children? Minor's consent to health care, treatment and research. *Soc Sci Med* **65**, 2272–83.

22. *Re R* [1991] 4 All ER 177 and *Re W* [1992] 4 All ER 627.

23. *Re L (A Minor)* [1998] 2 FLR 810 and *Re E (A Minor) (Wardship: Medical Treatment)* [1993] 1 FLR 386 each illustrates this point.

24. See Mental Capacity Act 2005, Code of Practice (2007). Chapter 12. London: HMSO. Available at: http://webarchive.nationalarchives.gov.uk/+/http://www.justice.gov.uk/docs/mca-cp.pdf.

25. See http://www.guardian.co.uk/uk/2009/jul/21/hannah-jones-heart-transplant.

26. Sexual Offences Act 2003.

27. See, for example, London Safeguarding Children Board (2011). *London Child Protection Procedures*, 4th edn, section 5.42. London: London Safeguarding Children Board. Available at: http://londonscb.gov.uk/procedures/.

28. See Rogstad, K., Thomas A., Williams, W. *et al.* (2010). *UK National Guideline on the Management of Sexually Transmitted Infections and Related Conditions in Young People 2010.* Clinical Effectiveness Group British Association for Sexual Health and HIV. Available at: http://www.bashh.org/documents/2674; HM Government (2010). *Working Together to Safeguard Children: a Guide to Inter-agency Working to Safeguard and Promote the Welfare of Children.* London: Department for Children, Schools and Families. Available at: http://www.education.gov.uk/publications/eOrderingDownload/00305-2010DOM-EN-v3.pdf.

29. See Dresser, R. S. (2007). Treatment decisions for incapacitated patients. In R. Ashcroft, A. Dawson, H. Draper and J. McMillan, eds., *Principles of Health Care Ethics*, 2nd edn, pp. 305–310. Chichester: Wiley.

30. Further cases of this type, with analysis, can be found in Brauner, D., Cameron Muir, J. and Sachs, G.(2000). Treating non-dementia patients' illnesses in patients with dementia. *JAMA* **283**, 3230–5.

31. Nicholson, T., Cutter, W. and Hotopf, M. (2008). Assessing mental capacity: the Mental Capacity Act. *BMJ* **336**, 322–5; Church, M. and Watts, S. (2007). Assessment of mental capacity: a flow chart guide. *Psych Bulletin* **31**, 304–7.

32. See Mental Capacity Act 2005, Code of Practice (2007). London: HMSO. Available at: http://webarchive.nationalarchives.gov.uk/+/http://www.justice.gov.uk/docs/mca-cp.pdf. and http://webarchive.nationalarchives.gov.uk/+/www.dh.gov.uk/en/SocialCare/Deliveringadultsocialcare/MentalCapacity/IMCA/DH_074510 for training materials.

33. See http://www.justice.gov.uk/global/forms/opg/lasting-power-of-attorney/index.htm for details of the UK system, administered by the Office of the Public Guardian.

34. A good review is to be found by Brock, D. (2007). Patient competence and surrogate decision-making. In R. M. Rhodes, L. P. Francis and A. Silvers, eds., *Blackwell Guide to Medical Ethics*, pp. 128–141. Oxford: Blackwell.

35. Buchanan, A. (2004). Mental capacity, legal competence and consent to treatment. *J Royal Soc Med* **97**, 415–20.

36. Seedhouse, D. (1998). *Ethics: the Heart of Health Care*, 2nd edn. Chichester: Wiley.

37. A fine description of this area lies in the Nuffield Council publication *Dementia: Ethical Issues*. Nuffield Council on Bioethics (2009). See also European Consensus Dementia Network (edited by G. Stoppe) (2007). *Competence Assessment in Dementia*. Berlin: Springer.

Chapter 3

Putting the informed into consent: information and decision-making

Introduction

This chapter will explore the element of consent that is probably most familiar to readers: information. The term 'informed consent' is commonplace (and sometimes afforded legal meaning that it does not have in the UK). Even if someone is not well-versed in the finer details of consent, it is likely that the vast majority of people understand that for consent to be meaningful there must be some sort of exchange of information. It is rare, in either our professional or personal lives, that we are content to agree blindly to a proposal without first finding out more and perhaps exploring the options in greater detail. It is a natural human instinct to seek information to help in making choices and taking decisions. The questions relating to sharing information have formed a significant part of the common law (or cases) that exist about consent and also the guidance on consent that is published by professional bodies such as the General Medical Council (GMC)[1] and Royal Colleges. An appreciation of the role of information is central both to a sound understanding of the concept of consent and its effective enactment in the clinical environment.

This chapter of the book will explore, in detail and with clinical examples, what it means to seek and obtain consent that is properly informed. The chapter aims to move beyond the somewhat mechanistic notion of 'information transfer' to consider why information is considered an important element of meaningful consent, what constitutes information, who might be responsible for sharing information with a patient (or potential patient) and how the requirement that consent should be informed can be best managed in the day-to-day demands of a busy clinical practice.

Why is information important?

Information is at the heart of consent. Unsurprisingly, one of the principal reasons for sharing information with patients is to support decision-making and choices. It is assumed that accurate, well-communicated information enables people to understand what is happening and what the available options might be. A good clinician will explain why treatment is indicated, what the treatment comprises and how it works, and he or she is also likely to give the patient the context for making a decision. That context might include discussion of alternatives and the advantages and drawbacks of the various options mentioned in the conversation. It is therefore natural to conclude that one of the ethical justifications for sharing information as part of the consent process is that it facilitates autonomy and contributes to better decision-making.

There are other, less well-explored ethical reasons for sharing information with patients. When a clinician takes the time to talk to a patient, they also take the time to get to know their patient a little better. By exploring some or all of the investigation of symptoms, potential diagnoses, possible treatments and outcomes, a clinician will learn more about what priorities, values, concerns, hopes and fears a patient brings to the conversation. Trust, rapport and confidence in the therapeutic relationship are likely to develop from an open and honest exchange of information between professional and patient. A less well-known ethical framework that may be useful when thinking about information in its broader sense is the narrative-based approach.

How does it help to consider sharing information through the lens of a narrative-based approach to ethics? A narrative approach to ethics emphasizes the subjective experience and assumes that individuals experience health and illness differently.[2] Its starting point therefore is that the individualized, subjective, partial and personal are important in the consultation in general, and in sharing information specifically. Immediately, information provision for the purposes of consent ceases to be a process whereby an expert professional gives a passive patient a version of esoteric and inaccessible knowledge that it has taken a clinician years to acquire. That is not to say that there is no place for the specialist knowledge that a clinician brings to the consultation, but it is to argue that both clinician and patient are engaged in a shared endeavour where there is more than one way of knowing, experiencing and conceptualizing health and illness. The medical 'story' – history, examination, investigations, diagnosis, treatment – is but one story that should be shared. The patient's story (and not the version that is translated into a well-ordered 'history' to be shared with other professionals) is equally important and integral to meaningful consent. No longer is the clinician an expert vessel for the transfer of specialist knowledge to the non-participative patient. Rather, both patient and clinician are actively engaged in explaining, listening, negotiating and responding to each other in a shared and transformative process that affords each party respect and dignity.

The experience of hearing people's stories – really hearing them properly – is immeasurably valuable. Clinical practice and bioethics are problem-focused. From the earliest days, clinicians learn to sift information seeking key points, looking for patterns and listening for alarm bells. A skill quickly acquired and required in clinical training is the ability to present, and respond to, a 'case'. Clinicians swiftly learn how to translate unstructured descriptions into histories, disparate subjectivity into objectively discernible signs and emotions into manageable agendas. Consultation 'models' and mnemonics assist in navigating the messy and discomforting worlds of patients. Many clinicians have finely honed communication skills and an abundance of empathy, but even the best clinician can miss the multiple perspectives that imbue consent. Both the words, and the expression of words, matter when seeking consent. Yet healthcare professionals are adept at inferring, assuming and even imposing meaning: individual experience is quickly bundled up into concepts such as 'information transfer', 'risks and benefits' and 'best interests'. A patient's story is unique: it may be messy, changing, unclear and, at times, redolent with contradiction.

A narrative approach to seeking consent requires clinicians, patients and families to come together as equals and to share a common task, namely reflecting on, explaining and describing their experience, perspective and priorities. It is often an exercise in revealing that which is hidden, in sharing that which would otherwise not be known and in acknowledging diversity and occasionally disagreement. The 'information' component of valid consent is much more than a clinician telling a patient what a drug does or why a particular test is indicated. It is inherently embedded in a complex process where clinicians try to listen to every carefully chosen word and to engage with multiple meanings. When one is used to being the 'expert' dealing with that which appears 'routine', it is important to be reminded of the power of words and the value of subjectivity.

When thinking about information and the ways in which it is conceptualized, one might ask the question: 'Does familiarity breed consent?' There are different ways in which familiarity might influence how information and its role in seeking consent are understood. Firstly, there is familiarity with the process of consent itself. Whatever the specialty, most healthcare practitioners have a way of sharing information that is established and familiar. For example, it might be that a GP uses a particular form of words to explain a decision to refer a patient (both to the patient and in the referral letter to the specialist). Healthcare is increasingly systematized and mechanisms are routinely in place to structure how information is shared with patients. For instance, it might be that the doctor carrying out endoscopies relies on the clinic nurse to explain the procedure and ensure that standard forms have been signed. It is easy to overlook the fact that what is merely another working day for the professional is likely to be a 'red-letter' day for the patient who may have had the appointment marked on their calendar for some time and made special arrangements to attend. A 'routine appointment' is rarely part of a patient's routine.

The second way in which familiarity can shape the provision of information is when a clinician gets to know a patient over time. The way in which information is conceptualized at the beginning of a therapeutic relationship may differ from the way in which it evolves over time. A long-standing history of working with a patient can be an asset and can contribute to trust and a strong relationship. Many readers will be able to recall times when knowing an individual patient well has enhanced clinical care. Indeed, in the UK, one of the often-heard criticisms of recent healthcare reform is that continuity of care, in both the primary and secondary care settings, is increasingly hard to find. Yet familiarity can also lead to shortcuts or misunderstanding about why information continues to matter. If someone has had the same procedure or treatment over a period of time, they have a different experience from that of a 'novice' patient. It can be all too easy to assume and anticipate, rather than to ask and explore. A narrow understanding of information might mean that a clinician fails to grasp how a patient's interests and wishes change over time. The sharing of information as part of the consent process is about clinician and patient discussing and reviewing their perspectives and experiences, without unduly privileging expert knowledge.

Another way in which to consider information that shifts the focus from outcomes to its inherent worth is to link it to the virtues one might expect a practitioner to bring to the act of seeking and obtaining consent. A virtue-based approach to consent places the emphasis on the characteristics or traits that we would like a clinician to demonstrate. So, in thinking about information, a virtue-based approach that values honesty, integrity, reliability, patience, courage, altruism and compassion will lead to the belief that doctor and patient should speak truthfully without shirking from difficult conversations, that it is the patient who is the centre of the consultation and that a clinician should be as alert to the emotional and social impact of disease and its treatment as to the scientific facts relating to diagnosis and treatment. It is an approach that, like the narrative-based approach, serves as a reminder that seeking consent is an inherently human endeavour, and the ethical challenge is not to identify how statistically significant a risk has to be before it is disclosed but to focus on that essential humanity. It is by sharing information and adapting it according to the needs, interests and priorities of individual patients that clinicians foster autonomy and give meaning to familiar terms such as choice, trust and care.

Having argued that there are multiple types of 'information' to be negotiated and shared between clinician and patient, what are the implications when a patient makes it clear that he or she does not wish to receive the amount or type of information that a clinician would routinely provide? Is it possible for a patient to insist on being uninformed?

Consider the scenario below.

Mr Adam Maitland is a 48-year-old accountant. He is due to have non-emergency surgery for a hernia repair. When seen by the anaesthetist, Dr Hansen, he explains that he does not wish to receive any information relating to the risks and benefits of a general anaesthetic versus a spinal anaesthetic. He would like Dr Hansen to decide what is best and to choose for him; after all, '… *she's the one who went to medical school.*'

One might argue that Mr Maitland is exercising his autonomy. As we have seen, the principle of patient autonomy in Western ethics has been argued by some to be pre-eminent.[3] However, that is a claim that warrants further interrogation. Autonomy is not merely a synonym for unfettered freedom and choice in all healthcare encounters. Such a conclusion depends on a simplistic misinterpretation of, and response to, the concept of autonomy, both personal and professional. It does not follow that patient autonomy, if not respected absolutely, is inevitably sacrificed at the altar of paternalistic medical authority.

For autonomy to have ethical value, it has to be something that is developed or facilitated by the exchange of information. To give meaning to autonomy does not translate as simply accepting that which any patient may choose. Rather, it is a moral concept that assumes that self-determination depends, to some extent, on active participation in exploring choices. Uninformed and unscrutinized resistance to any notion of choice is not, by definition, a choice. Dr Hansen has choices too. She might find Mr Maitland's point blank refusal to engage with her frustrating and puzzling. She may decide that she is going to invoke professional guidance to insist that she has to explain the anaesthetic options to Mr Maitland whether he likes it or not. To do so would, of course, be a somewhat ironic insistence on compulsory autonomy. In this situation, it is not whether Mr Maitland's autonomy takes priority over Dr Hansen's professional autonomy that is the question, but how autonomy can be facilitated, developed, maximized and shared by the parties and the specific role of information in so doing. As such, 'autonomy' (personal or professional) is not something to be fought over but a common aim of clinician and patient in which sharing contrasting, or even conflicting, perspectives allows for and demands dialogue, discussion and decision-making based on mutual respect and increased understanding.

The preferred route might be to explore why Mr Maitland is so reluctant to receive information. What is it that he is expecting to hear? If, as seems likely from the vignette, he is anticipating a discussion of the risks and potential harms that might attach to surgery, his request may be driven by a fear that is entirely understandable. A frightened or anxious patient who has perhaps spent several weeks worrying about an operation may well be resistant to receiving information if it is understood solely as a matter of setting out the risks and benefits. Perhaps readers who studiously avoid watching the safety briefing on airplanes or who prefer not to read reports of the possibilities and risks of natural disasters, economic downturns or road traffic accidents can understand what might be motivating Mr Maitland's reluctance to hear from Dr Hansen what risks he is facing.

Dr Hansen and Mr Maitland are demonstrating why the conceptualization of information and its perceived significance to consent matters. Dr Hansen quite naturally is preparing to do something that she does daily, namely to present the principal risks and potential benefits of types of anaesthesia to a patient. Mr Maitland is preparing to do something that he has never done before and that is a particularly significant event in his life. The information that Dr Hansen has to share is important, but so too is Mr Maitland's perspective, and thus far she has not enquired what he thinks, feels or fears about the surgery. It is unsurprising, perhaps, that this unspoken mismatch has led to an apparent information stalemate.

Given the relative positions of Dr Hansen and Mr Maitland, what does it mean to foster patient autonomy and what are the implications for the ways in which information is understood? Perhaps, first it means rejecting a notion of autonomy that is constructed in an artificially binary way, as an 'all or nothing' choice in which Dr Hansen either gives Mr Maitland the standard information or she doesn't. Meaningful choices cannot be made in a vacuum – Mr Maitland's perspective has to be explored and, in so far as is possible, understood by Dr Hansen. Her priority may be the discussion of risks and benefits with a view to decision-making, but, for whatever reason, that priority is not shared by Mr Maitland[4] and she needs to explore why. To reduce the complexity of the variables that might be influencing Mr Maitland to a competition between doctor and patient choice is simplistic, unhelpful and ultimately counter-therapeutic. Once autonomy is reinterpreted for both Dr Hansen and Mr Maitland as a common process in which information is equitably exchanged with the shared aim of improving health (rather than merely authorizing surgery with a particular anaesthetic), the issue of which party's preference should 'trump' the other party's preference in the consultation becomes redundant. It is not about either Mr Maitland or Dr Hansen 'defending' their position but exploring, and explaining, the differences in their respective perspectives. To do so is to create, perpetuate and respect autonomy in a meaningful and ethically sustainable way.

To return to the specific example, what should Dr Hansen do? Firstly, she needs to talk to Mr Maitland about why he does not want to receive any information and specifically explore what information he is refusing so vehemently. Such a discussion opens the door to a shared understanding of information that affords equal status to the perspectives of both parties. From both the sharing of information and the elucidation of how each person is interpreting the 'information' comes awareness and challenging of assumptions. The 'problem' can be reframed: no longer is it a question of frustration at conflicting professional and personal wishes; instead it becomes a process of understanding better the perspectives of both parties and working together in the interests of the patient.

The exchange of information is the ultimate ethical tool, and without it, discussions of autonomy are meaningless. Of course, even after exploring patient and professional preferences, difference may still remain between Dr Hansen and Mr Maitland. However, the scene has been set for negotiation and compromise. As this scenario involves non-urgent surgery, Dr Hansen and Mr Maitland have time to explore the options. It may mean that Dr Hansen decides to proceed without giving as much information as she would routinely do: however, it is likely that she will do so feeling more comfortable with their decision having heard why it is that Mr Maitland is so reluctant to hear about different anaesthesia options.[5] Conversely, Dr Hansen may decide that she will gently but firmly explain the relative risks and benefits of anaesthesia as part of a wider conversation with her patient, but Mr Maitland is more likely to understand why she has done so rather than feeling that the doctor has exercised her authority and is expressing disapproval of his 'non-cooperation'.

Look who's talking: who should provide information?

The preceding section of this chapter has argued that it is important that information is understood as incorporating different perspectives, individual experiences and personal values, as well as the expert, professional knowledge that is usually considered to constitute the 'informed' part of consent. The question of who talks to the patient and when is significant when considering what it means for consent to be informed. Healthcare is delivered by teams of people working on a shift basis, which has implications for informing patients as part of the process of seeking and obtaining consent. Consider the following scenario.

> Dr Anderson is a Foundation year doctor working on a general medical team. He graduated from medical school approximately 6 months ago. He is currently the most junior member of the clinical team. Mrs Lucy Barrington is scheduled to have an adrenocorticotrophic hormone (ACTH) stimulation (Synacthen) test because it is thought that she might have Addison's disease. Dr Anderson has been asked to obtain Mrs Barrington's consent by his Registrar.

Dr Anderson's ability to give Mrs Barrington the information she requires is dependent on both his knowledge about the specific test and its clinical relevance, and his clinical consultation skills. Dr Anderson has been charged with a task that goes beyond a textbook recitation of the indications for, and process of, an ACTH stimulation test. He has to engage with Mrs Barrington and develop sufficient rapport to enable him to respond to her concerns, questions and priorities so as to support her in coming to a decision.

Professional bodies, such as the GMC in the UK, recognize in their guidance on consent that it may not always be possible for the doctor undertaking a specific procedure to discuss it personally with the patient. The GMC guidance supports the delegation of the responsibility for seeking consent to a colleague provided that '*the person is suitably trained and qualified and has sufficient knowledge of the proposed investigation or treatment and understands the risks involved.*[6] The same guidance, however, emphasizes that the clinician who is carrying out the investigation or procedure remains responsible for ensuring that the patient has been given enough time and information to make a choice.[7]

Dr Anderson is therefore being asked to do something that is acceptable, provided he is supported by, and accountable to, his registrar and ultimately a consultant in overall charge of the team. Indeed, Dr Anderson is part of a long tradition in which doctors in training are asked to seek and obtain consent. Such experience has often been perceived as an important part of clinical training that develops communication skills, enhances a junior doctor's clinical knowledge of a specific procedure or intervention, and fosters insight into patient priorities and concerns. Naturally, for there to be a genuinely educational benefit from participating in seeking consent, Dr Anderson would have some understanding of what it means to do the task 'well' and would receive constructive feedback on how he does in seeking consent from Mrs Barrington. The educational value of involving junior members of the team in seeking consent is a point that is taken up by the GMC in its guidance for recently qualified doctors and stresses the need for appropriate guidance, support and supervision as clinicians in training take on increasing responsibility in practice.[8] Increasingly, healthcare training recognizes the value of structured learning in practice and makes explicit that which had previously been assumed or implicit in clinical training. For example, foundation schools commonly provide guidance on the role of junior doctors in seeking consent, emphasizing that the early years of training provide an opportunity to develop good habits in relation to seeking consent.[9] Consent is not just an abstract ethico-legal construct. It is a clinical competence that depends on developing skills in listening, information-sharing, demonstrating empathy and negotiation. Just as one would not expect an inexperienced or newly qualified clinician to be able to perform a procedure or manage a complex patient without supervision, support and constructive feedback, so too becoming skilled in seeking consent depends on much more than simply having a grasp of the technical details of whatever procedure or treatment is under consideration. Fortunately, those responsible for overseeing clinical training are increasingly aware of the value of, and process involved in, developing the ability of newly qualified practitioners both to seek consent properly and to resist inappropriate requests to seek consent.

A second area where the identity of the person providing information can be relevant is where different members of a professional team take on particular roles. If clinical work is organized so that a particular individual is responsible for seeking consent but the clinician actually providing treatment is someone else, it is important to consider how the provision of information and responses to patient concerns are being managed. Consider the scenario below.

Miss Nina Briers is an anaesthetic nurse practitioner. She has been appointed to obtain anaesthetic consent prior to elective surgery. Patients are admitted over the course of the day for surgery. By giving the task of seeking consent to Miss Briers rather than the anaesthetist, interruptions to the operating list are avoided. Mr Michael O'Donnell is to have surgery on his bowel for ulcerative colitis and will require a general anaesthetic with the option of an epidural for analgesia in the post-operative period.

The process of seeking and obtaining surgical consent has been the subject of specific attention in both the clinical and ethico-legal literature for some time.[10] The way in which the roles in surgery are divided between different professionals makes it a particular environment in which to consider the provision of information and, ultimately, what constitutes meaningful consent. Traditionally, the surgeon was responsible for the operation and the anaesthetist responsible for the anaesthetic. Pre-operative discussions took place in a surgical outpatient clinic and there was usually a period of time between the substantive discussion of the procedure and signing a consent form on the morning of surgery. Such practice, whilst fitting with the organization and administration of surgery, was not considered good practice in relation to sharing information and seeking consent.[11] As shall be discussed in Chapter 5, consent is a process and, in relation to the provision of information exchange, a one-off appointment in an outpatient clinic and a pre-operative request for a signature on a consent form were not conducive to creating opportunities to reflect on the information provided, ask questions, discuss the options with family and come to a considered decision.

If one accepts, as has been argued in this chapter, that the concept of information is more than merely the transfer of expert knowledge about risks and benefits, the arguments in support of a professional who is specifically charged with talking to patients, exploring their priorities and responding to individual concerns may be persuasive. No longer is the sole focus of the consultation a medically or surgically dominated meeting but an opportunity for the patient and a professional to negotiate both the details of the proposed surgery and, crucially, what those details mean to the person preparing to undergo that surgery.[12] A sound knowledge of medicine or surgery may be necessary, but it is insufficient. Naturally, there are conditions that anyone working in the role of the anaesthetic nurse practitioner, like Miss Briers in the scenario above, must fulfil. Firstly, she needs to have sufficient knowledge of anaesthesia to provide sufficient information to Mr O'Donnell. In this scenario, Miss Briers must be adequately trained to discuss analgesic options and the risks and benefits of an epidural. Her knowledge must also, crucially, include an awareness of the limits of her knowledge; she must know what she does not know and when to refer for further advice, clarification or information. Secondly,

Miss Briers must, like anyone working with patients, understand the process of seeking and obtaining consent. Thirdly, there should, as with any clinical work, be some way of evaluating and reviewing the effects of her work on the overall performance of the clinical team.[13]

For nurse-led consent to work, it has to be understood by both patient and clinicians as one element in a team approach to supporting patient decision-making. Most, if not all, nurse-led consent systems operate within the boundaries of well-delineated protocols with clearly stated exclusions and conditions.[14] It is important that Miss Briers is not perceived by her colleagues as the 'consent technician' or 'the person who talks to the patients'. Responsibility for consent is shared by all those involved in Mr O'Donnell's care. It is not that consent has been 'delegated' but that it is being overtly recognized as shared within the clinical team, with Miss Briers having a specific part to play particularly in relation to beginning to discuss what information Mr O'Donnell needs to give consent. Moral responsibility for consent is informed by, but not defined by, a professional role. Miss Briers has a particular role in initiating a conversation with Mr O'Donnell and engaging in meaningful discussion about what is proposed, but her work does not alter the responsibility of either the anaesthetist or the surgeon involved in Mr O'Donnell's care.

Lest the discussion thus far appears naïve, it should be noted that the increase in nurse-led services has sometimes been prompted by considerations that have nothing to do with the quality of information received by patients or the process of seeking consent. Undoubtedly, expanding the role of professional staff other than doctors has been a theme in healthcare policy for over a decade. In the policy literature,[15] increased efficiency,[16] resource savings, reductions in medical staff hours and changes to shift patterns have all been invoked as reasons to support nurse-led services. Indeed, in some jurisdictions, use is being made of technology to facilitate the provision of information with patients both prior to, and after, surgery.[17]

Whatever the reasons for Miss Briers being in the role she has, there may be disadvantages to consider. In the scenario presented, for example, it may be disconcerting for Mr O'Donnell to meet the anaesthetist for the first time in the anaesthetic room, although, assuming that Miss Briers has done her job well, he should understand the role of the anaesthetist in seeking consent and have had the opportunity to speak to him or her should he so wish prior to admission. Likewise, if the anaesthetist fulfils his or her professional role, consent will not be deemed to be a mere formality but a process in which the anaesthetist builds on the foundations laid by Miss Briers and her interaction with Mr O'Donnell.

Some readers may have reservations about the safety of such an approach. After all, whilst serious complications secondary to anaesthesia are rare, when they do occur such complications can have a significant impact on patient morbidity. Although it is relatively early days in the evolution of approaches to consent that are led by professionals other than doctors, there is evidence that most, if not all, protocols are both written and evaluated with patient safety in mind.[18]

As healthcare evolves, the question of who is, and should be, providing information to patients is likely to be a recurrent theme. It is likely that individual clinicians and their patients will respond differently to the changing nature of professional roles and the impact on sharing information. There will be inevitable variation of practice depending on the country, specialty and locality of the clinical service in which one is working. However, irrespective of role, professional identity or geographical location, there are common factors that apply to the provision of information. Firstly, the person providing the information should be in a position to share not only what is known but also what is unknown. That uncertainty may be because of the particular expertise or training of the clinician, or it may be that the evidence base itself is partial. Nonetheless, anyone who is providing information should be aware of the limits of what is known and what he or she knows as an individual practitioner. Secondly, each professional is contributing to a team endeavour and it is essential that one has insight into one's particular contribution to the overall process of seeking consent and providing clinical care. That insight, and an explanation of where an individual 'sits' in the overarching provision of care, should be shared with the patient, who should understand who in the clinical team does what, when, why and how. Thirdly, and related to insight into one's role, information must be understood to include, but not be defined by, particular expertise. If information is to be useful to a particular patient, it must be tailored and flexible. The verb of choice is 'exchange' rather than 'transfer' when talking about information and consent. Finally, a collaborative approach that puts the interests of the patient before professional territory and tribal allegiance is essential for disseminated models of information provision and consent to work.

How much information?

A common preoccupation for both patients and clinicians alike is how much information is sufficient for the purposes of consent. Much practical teaching on consent focuses, perhaps too much, on the quantity of information, sometimes at the expense of highlighting the significance of the quality of information shared with patients. The language that is used to described how much information should be shared can be confusing with adjectives like 'sufficient', 'reasonable', 'material', 'serious' and 'significant' used interchangeably, yet also differently, in both the literature and clinical practice.

Inevitably, both the amount and type of information that clinicians share with patients is important. Information is significant in both objective and subjective ways when seeking consent. Objectively, it matters that everyone has the opportunity to make a decision by receiving information that is accurate, honest and captures the essence of a proposed intervention or course of treatment. Subjectively, patients need information that is relevant to them, specific and responsive to their own particular concerns and priorities. This combination of information that is both objectively sound and subjectively meaningful is what makes the determination of the right amount and type of information a complex clinical challenge. There will be pieces of information that are applicable to anyone considering a particular procedure or medication and then there is information that matters specifically or uniquely to the individual patient. Each time a clinician shares information with, and seeks consent from, a new patient, it is likely to differ, perhaps only marginally but nonetheless perceptibly, from previous occasions. Such divergence in the content and form of information is not only natural, it is ethically desirable because, assuming it is informed by the context, priorities and individual features of the patient, it demonstrates that information is not being 'transferred' or 'given' routinely and unthinkingly but that information is being shared and adapted, autonomy fostered and meaningful consent sought.

Nonetheless, there is guidance available about the type and extent of information that should be shared with patients. Firstly, there is professional guidance, which tends to take a patient-centred approach (which is, of course, congruent with its overarching values and reflects the primary task, which is to serve and, where required, protect patients). The advice from professional bodies, such as the GMC in the UK, is to be led by the patient.[19] It will probably not be a surprise to readers that we consider this approach to have much to commend it. The preceding and subsequent discussions in this book argue that a patient-led approach to seeking and obtaining consent is ethically and clinically desirable. It is an approach that requires attention to partnership and negotiation. It facilitates meaningful autonomous decision-making where someone has capacity and informs the determination of best interests where a patient lacks capacity to make his or her own choices. A patient-oriented approach reflects the nuances and complexities of clinical consultations allowing for multiple ways of knowing and experiencing healthcare. From a virtue ethics perspective, by focusing on the patient, a professional is likely to be acting with compassion, patience, humility, integrity, openness and a desire to serve.

The normative appeal of patient-led information-sharing may be frustrated by the realities of clinical practice where practical limitations constrain the amount of time available to provide information that attends to both the subjective and objective elements sought and valued by different patients. Those practical limitations are real and must be factored in to any discussion about consent. Nonetheless, it may well be an ethical 'false economy' to hasten or curtail the information-sharing element of a consultation. If trust, an effective therapeutic alliance and the right to self-determination are predicated on seeking and obtaining meaningful consent, this would seem to be a part of clinical work that should not be rushed; the stakes are simply too high. Just as the neurosurgeon accepts that the delicate and lengthy operation will take a certain amount of time, perhaps collectively clinicians should accept that sharing information will, sometimes and not always, take longer than they might previously have accepted or learned. Moreover, to share information effectively with patients does not necessarily mean taking longer. It is more likely to mean that different skills are used, particularly in listening, responding, allowing silence and observing verbal and non-verbal cues, but not that the consultation need necessarily be longer. Small changes to routine can have significant effects without inevitably slowing an already over-stretched system.

In common with most areas of clinical practice, the law can both shape and distort how information is understood in relation to consent. Just as in all other aspects of practice, professionals owe a duty of care to patients to seek and obtain consent to an acceptable standard, otherwise they may be held to be negligent. In other words, a negligently sought or obtained consent is no different from a negligently performed examination, procedure or prescription. An action in negligence[20] comprises three elements, namely:

1. A duty of care between claimant and defendant.
2. A breach, by an act or omission, that falls below the standard of care expected.
3. Causation, i.e. the breach resulted in loss or damage to the claimant that was reasonably proximate.

As regards sharing information for the purposes of consent, a duty of care exists between healthcare professionals and patients.[21] It is the questions of the standard of care provided and causation (in fact and in law) that are likely to form the 'legal meat' of a claim in negligence. A claim may be predicated solely on the basis of the consent sought and obtained. In other words, it is possible for a patient to succeed in a negligence action for inadequate consent even where the procedure or treatment was appropriate and competently provided. All of which prompts the question of what the standard of care is for clinicians providing information with the purpose of seeking consent?

In the UK, the standard of care is common to all negligence claims. For many years, the courts considered whether a defendant had behaved in a way that accorded with a responsible body of professional opinion. It need not be a majority opinion, but it does need to be considered reasonable and not reflect a perverse or esoteric professional perspective. This way of determining the standards of care was known as the '*Bolam* test' after the case in which it was first articulated.[22] In practice, for matters of clinical judgement, an expert or number of experts would advise the courts on the acceptability or otherwise of a defendant's conduct. Therefore, on application of the *Bolam* test, if an expert witness stated that a clinician's actions (or omissions) were those of a reasonable practitioner, it was most unlikely that he or she would be found negligent.

The *Bolam* test was criticized by those who believed that it invested the power to make determinative judgement in medical opinion (as represented by medically qualified expert witnesses).[23] The test was also perceived as flawed because it equated commonly accepted practice with acceptable practice.[24]

At the end of the twentieth century, the courts showed signs of dissatisfaction with the role of experts and its effect on standards of care. In 1997, in the case of *Bolitho v. City and Hackney Health Authority*,[25] the House of Lords introduced a new element to the assessment of standards of care. The Lords held that a court was not bound to accept that a doctor had not been negligent merely because expert opinion affirmed that a defendant's actions accorded with those of a responsible body of his peers. The House stated that, in order to be judged 'reasonable', a defendant's actions (and the expert's opinion of those actions) should be capable of withstanding logical analysis by the court. Thus, for the first time, there was a clear statement by the most senior members of the judiciary that courts should scrutinize medical opinion rather than simply accept the assessments of expert witnesses. The decision generated much comment in the professional and academic literature and was interpreted (and indeed welcomed) by many as marking the demise of the power of the medical profession to determine an appropriate standard of care.[26] However, in practice, only a negligible number of cases will produce expert opinions that are so unreasonable that they do not withstand logical analysis. For the purposes of considering standards relating to information-sharing and consent, *Bolitho* is significant because it indicates that the interpretation of guidance on consent is not the preserve of experts but something on which the court can and, where appropriate, will comment. It is, along with the approach of professional guidelines on consent, another endorsement of sharing information and seeking consent in a way that is patient-centred, equal and considered.

In addition to the potential for a claim in negligence, poorly or inadequately obtained consent can also amount to battery or assault.[27] It is not necessary for the claimant to prove loss or harm in making a claim. The claims are predicated on the physical touch, or attempted touch, of another person without permission, i.e. consent. It does not matter if the aim of touching was therapeutic or beneficial; the body is deemed to be inviolate at law. As has already been discussed, permission or consent may be express for example by signing a consent form, or implied by virtue of a patient's actions, such as offering an arm for a blood test or stepping into an X-ray room. Although the UK does not have a legal concept of 'informed consent' (information is but one of the elements of legally valid consent), in practice it is often the absence or poor quality of information that informs the evaluation of whether consent has been properly obtained, and therefore whether an action for battery will succeed. A claim will be brought on the basis of a patient's perception. If information is understood to encompass a process by which professional and personal perspectives are exchanged, individual context explored and a constructive dialogue developed, clinicians are less likely to find themselves misunderstood and, worse still, the subject of legal action.

In most areas of our lives, people care about how they are perceived and heard: patients and doctors in the consultation are no different, and this simplicity captures what it means to share information. Whilst there may be apparently conflicting guidance about risk disclosure and legal urban myths that are passed between generations of professionals about particular percentages and the severity of potential risks, the essence of consent requires only that both patient and professional attend to how they, and the information they share, are perceived and heard.

What don't you know? Uncertainty and consent

Renee Fox,[28] in her seminal study of medical training and practice, argued that uncertainty in medicine is inevitable and falls into two categories. The first refers to the limitations of an individual doctor's knowledge; the second (and more significant) describes the intrinsically limited nature of medical knowledge itself. Recently, Fox revisited uncertainty in medicine and its relationship to basic science to elucidate what she describes as 'epistemological uncertainty' in which scientific 'evidence' is invoked to create an illusory certainty.[29] Medicine is incomplete, controversial and contested, and there remains an infinite number of unanswered, and perhaps unanswerable, questions. In relation to consent, the inherent uncertainty of medicine, scientific knowledge and the mysteries of healthcare are as relevant to a discussion of information as accounts of risks and benefits.

Uncertainty is noteworthy in another sense: it is a rare example of a concept that sociologists, philosophers and the healthcare professions agree is fundamental to the daily work of practising clinicians. Most practitioners will know the indefinable mixture of intuition, experience and expertise that they bring to their clinical practice. It has been beautifully described by Kathryn Hunter as the '*paradox of epistemological naïveté*' that requires clinicians simultaneously to draw on hermeneutic wisdom while supporting the scientific credentials of medicine.[30] It is dynamic tension between the boundaries of the epistemological ideal of medicine as a well-delineated science and the ever-present creeping challenge of medical ambiguity, surprise, diversity and confusion that renders the sharing of information for the purposes of seeking consent so complex. Uncertainty must be recognized, explained and managed just like any other aspect of information that is relevant to a person making a decision about healthcare. The articulation and negotiation of uncertainty is at the core of what it means to be a practising clinician and yet it rarely appears in discussions of information-sharing and consent.

How then can uncertainty, and its implications for consent, be managed in clinical practice? Perhaps the most obvious protective effect for both patient and professional comes from practitioners having an awareness of the limitations of knowledge and a willingness to be open about those limitations. It is not easy to steer a course between risk, patient preferences, biomedical knowledge and clinical uncertainty. A conceptualization of information shared for the purposes of consent that requires clinicians to think both about what is known and unknown and how that might affect a patient's decision is invaluable. An honest exchange allows the patient to take, or at least share, the burden of uncertainty, giving individuals the opportunity to explain their personal tolerance for uncertainties and risks as they make a decision about their healthcare.

Consider the scenario below.

> Christopher Newman is 8 years old and arrives at his local GP surgery with his father. Christopher has acute ear ache. Dr Davison examines Christopher and concludes that he has acute otitis media. Dr Davison notes that Christopher is allergic to penicillin. Dr Davison explains the diagnosis to Christopher and his father; he explains that it is likely to be viral but may not be, in which case there might be a place for antibiotic treatment. Mr Newman appears confused and Dr Davison explains the concept of the 'number needed to treat' as applied to acute otitis media. He says that research indicates that one would need to treat 100 children like Christopher to help ten get better, or at least to shorten the illness from 7 to 3 days. During treatment of the 100 children, some may get diarrhoea and other side effects.
>
> Christopher's father seems nonplussed by Dr Davison's explanation and asks, 'Will treatment help or not?'

The rather stylized scenario above demonstrates how the best intentions of the clinician to share information where the outcome is uncertain can confuse rather than clarify. Despite his best efforts, it seems Dr Davison has only managed to puzzle Mr Newman. We may draw several conclusions from the scenario. Firstly, it looks as though the exploration of the concept of numbers needed to treat (NNT) has backfired in that, as an elucidation of uncertainty, it has neither resonated with, nor improved the understanding of, Mr Newman. For many clinicians, NNT is nothing more complex than a statistical truism, built on the empirical evidence about the treatment of acute otitis media. However, it may be an alien idea to those who are unfamiliar with the ways in which clinical evidence is interpreted to inform prescribing decisions.[31] Words about risk are inherently risky. Expressions such as 'failure of procedure' or 'damage to adjacent structures' that are often used in clinical practice may carry a range of meanings and risk multiple interpretations and misinterpretations. Concepts that are grist to the clinical mill such as 'normal variant', 'reference range', 'soft marker' and 'statistical significance' are heard more often than they are well explained in the consultation. Such concepts are often invoked to delineate the boundaries of uncertainty, or at least the limits of tolerable uncertainty. However, if patients are never introduced to the notion that the medicine is an uncertain endeavour, it is unsurprising that they do not quickly engage with the tools professionals use to manage that uncertainty in practice.

It might be felt that the information Dr Davison provided to Mr Newman and Christopher in the scenario above is detailed, perhaps too detailed, whilst doing little to explain the inevitability of the uncertainty of treatment outcome. It was perhaps a poor choice by Dr Davison, and it may be that something simpler may have achieved his aim of explaining to Mr Newman why the prescribing of antibiotics is not necessarily going to be an effective intervention. For example, he might have explained that most otitis media is viral rather than bacterial in origin. As antibiotics will treat only bacterial infections and all antibiotics have side effects, inevitably some people will experience side effects without experiencing the benefits of the prescribed drug.

Dr Davison should not be criticized for apparently getting it wrong with Mr Newman. We all express ourselves poorly at times, and most of us have both misunderstood and been misunderstood. Unfortunately, merely because one says something, it does not mean that the person to whom one has spoken has understood what was said or intended. Perhaps it was a mistake for Dr Davison to introduce specific figures into the consultation. It may have been preferable for Dr Davison to explain what he would consider to be in Christopher's best interests using simpler concepts to support his assessment of the situation and being honest about the inherent uncertainty of determining whether Christopher has a viral or bacterial infection. There is no shame in getting the explanation wrong when talking to a patient. However, it is problematic if the clinician either does not register that his or her best efforts at effective communication have gone awry or does not respond to the cues that the patient is bemused or otherwise unconvinced by the explanation. At first sight, it may appear that Dr Davison is engaged in a routine and commonplace clinical task: the treatment of an ear infection in a child. Yet underpinning the consultation are fundamental concepts that go to the heart of both ethics and the epistemo-logical basis of medicine. Dr Davison is juggling multiple ways of knowing: Christopher's reported symptoms, Mr Newman's observations of his son whom he sees daily, evidence from population data about antibiotic treatment for otitis media, the specific clinical contraindication to prescribing penicillin for Christopher and his own clinical judgement and intuition. His task is far from simple or routine. Dr Davison has, in the limited time available, to consider all those forms of knowledge and communicate his assessment of the situation to Mr Newman (who, lest we forget, is also likely to be juggling his own narratives, emotions and priorities, albeit perhaps in his head, while trying to listen to Dr Davison). It is little wonder the process sometimes goes awry! The ethical imperative is not to provide information perfectly at the first attempt on every occasion but to work hard, both to understand and to be understood, persevering to create the possibility of shared understanding.

What do you want to know that for? The purpose of information

Healthcare is naturally outcome-focused, and many clinicians are attracted to approaches to ethics that consider the consequences of a particular decision or action. Having argued earlier in this chapter that other ethical approaches might be useful when considering the value of information and its part in seeking consent, this section of the chapter now considers whether and how the purpose of discovering or disclosing information may inform the ethical analysis. When thinking about the impact (or otherwise) of the purpose of information, the example of consent and information in the field of clinical genetics is a thought-provoking starting point. Perhaps more than most specialties, in clinical genetics, information about the potential diagnoses can affect not only the individual patient but also other family members. Consider the scenario below.

> Mrs Connie Ruby is a 30-year-old woman who is worried about her family history and her susceptibility to breast cancer. She sees her primary care doctor to discuss these concerns. Dr Yterba takes a full three-generation family history, which reveals that Mrs Ruby has two first-degree relatives with breast cancer and two second-degree relatives similarly affected. The doctor consults the relevant guidelines and Mrs Ruby is classified as high risk. She is referred to genetic services where she undergoes genetic tests, revealing her *BRCA1* status. Dr Yterba and Mrs Ruby are discussing the implications of the news from the genetic testing and she mentions that she has a sister from whom she is estranged.

People have much more access to genetic information about themselves than was possible even a few years ago.[32] There are many commercial organizations now functioning that offer genomic risk assessments, based on cohort studies of associative single-nucleotide substitutions but of unclear clinical significance. In Mrs Ruby's case, the risk assessments are well defined: she is at high risk of developing breast and other cancers. Thus, she will be exposed to a great deal of complex numerical risk material as a result of her *BRCA1* gene status and may be considering many therapeutic options: from intensive supervision to bilateral mastectomy. Now, a certain proportion of the information that Mrs Ruby will encounter after her diagnosis will have been given to her prior to the genetic testing – it is good and accepted practice in clinical genetics to discuss the possible outcomes of testing as part of seeking consent. In some cases, such information at that stage may even have suggested to her that she should not proceed, for fear of exposure of the diagnosis.

The scenario presented, however, goes beyond the usual dyadic relationship of clinician and patient to introduce a third, absent party: her estranged sister who, on the facts given, is also at risk. We may ask whether this new person in the story should share the information too, so she may make her own decision about investigation. Two interlinked narratives therefore present themselves for consideration: how much information should be available to Mrs Ruby via primary care or specialist genetic services to support her decision-making about testing, and what should be done with any genetic information that has arisen as a result of providing care to Mrs Ruby? Is there any moral distinction to be drawn about the purpose for which such information might be used, i.e. diagnostically and/or therapeutically? In this sort of case, it is immediately obvious that consent to diagnostic processes can be more complex than consent to therapeutic processes. To return to the first scenario in this chapter, Mr Maitland as he consents, or otherwise, to the proposed hernia repair will be offered information and clinical support and thus he decides whether to proceed. After he has recovered from the procedure, the consent becomes a historical marker, among others, of his medical history. Diagnostic procedures are not time limited in this way and clearly can have many possible outcomes. In most situations where a diagnostic procedure is proposed, patients will have had an opportunity to discuss their presenting symptoms, the possible causes of their symptoms and perhaps the treatment options related to those causes. Much of that information is provisional, uncertain and contingent. In Mrs Ruby's case, these factors apply to the diagnostic process too, enlarged by the genetic context. Her doctors will have suspected from the adverse family history that a formal genetic cause such as *BRCA1* or *BRCA2* gene mutation may be underlying Mrs Ruby's presentation.

Mrs Ruby's case raises questions about the scope and purpose of genetic information. She has sought the information and, although we know little of her motives, we are told that she is concerned about her family history and her personal susceptibility to breast cancer. However, only she has sought the information. Her sister has not. There was no overt or sought 'purpose' in obtaining the genetic information about Mrs Ruby's estranged sister. It is akin to an 'incidental finding', albeit a finding with far from incidental implications. Ethical theory does not give a clear answer to these questions about the extent of the information sought or its potential reach. However, the absence of a determinative ethical answer does not mean that ethical analysis might not be helpful.

There are, as always in ethics, different ways of approaching the questions raised by Mrs Ruby's situation. Most commentators and clinicians would agree that, as she has sought this particular piece of genetic information, it should be disclosed to Mrs Ruby, even if the reasons for such a conclusion differ according to ethical preference. Someone arguing from a rights-based perspective might suggest that the genetic information about Mrs Ruby is profound and that she is entitled to be informed. A consequentialist might argue that Mrs Ruby's best chances of long-term survival demand the same. Neither of these arguments contributes very much to defining the degree of information we may argue as ethical. More persuasive might be respect for the principle of autonomy and, specifically, fostering Mrs Ruby's autonomy so that she can make important decisions for herself about the effect of this result, the implications for her children (should she either have, or be intending to have, any), the effect of this test result on her risk profile for other diseases, and so on.

Mrs Ruby's responses are likely to be framed as a question as the interrogative is often the preferred way for people to receive and process difficult information. There are good examples of how to translate complex, formal data into user-friendly form,[33] but it is suggested that information-sharing is best led by the patient, may take place over time and occurs in the context of an ongoing conversation between clinician and patient. It also demands certain behaviour on the part of the doctor: certainly the clinical skills of good communication and sensitivity but also the moral qualities (or virtues) of patience, honesty, respect and willingness to learn. It is by using these skills and demonstrating those qualities that Mrs Ruby and her clinical team can negotiate and renegotiate the purpose of sharing information.

However, what purpose might there be in disclosing the information discovered as part of the genetic testing of Mrs Ruby to her sister or beyond? There is a considerable body of literature available on the notion of duties in relation to adverse genetic information among families.[34] Rights arguments can be mustered on both sides of a dilemma where relatives might have access to genetic information emanating from an index case, as can arguments about best interests. Consensus, such as there is, seems to confer a duty to report such information on the index case personally, rather than any doctor involved with their care. There have been a few cases at law in the USA that are inconsistent[35] and do not add to the professional guidance at the time of writing. If one considers the purpose of the genetic information sought and obtained, perhaps the ethical picture becomes clearer. Mrs Ruby sought a test for herself. She neither considered nor involved her sister in her decision. It might be argued that she should have considered her sibling, but she did not. The purpose of testing was to provide information to Mrs Ruby. We have argued that the patient should lead in sharing information and integrating that information into his or her life. To remove that freedom from a patient and to insist on overriding a patient's purpose in seeking information would be to introduce a curious *ex post facto* element of paternalism.

In an ideal world, the information that Mrs Ruby shared with her GP and the genetic service prior to testing would have alerted her to the possibilities of the results having implications for others. It may be that Mrs Ruby's definition of 'others' no longer includes her estranged sister and that may be difficult for some to accept. We are not told whether she mentions her estranged sister in passing or more deliberately (and a psychoanalyst might suggest that no one, especially a relative, is ever 'mentioned in passing') during the consultation with her GP. It might be that, having been given the opportunity, her GP decides to explore with Mrs Ruby whether she has considered the possible implications of the test for all female relatives, including the estranged sister she mentions. Ultimately, Mrs Ruby may decide that news of a genetic test indicating susceptibility to cancer is not the best way to end an estrangement or she may decide that its import outweighs the history between her and her sibling. It is her decision to make. The boundaries of what should be done with the information provided by the genetic test are hers to draw. The clinical team involved has a responsibility to see that Mrs Ruby is able to make the best decisions possible and in a way that allows her to meet the intended purpose of her initial consultation; clinical information has to be integrated into real lives with the myriad complexities of human relationships, personal difference and individual priorities. It is that integration that provides common purpose.

Putting it all together: the essence of information

This chapter has suggested that the sharing of information for the purposes of consent is much more than merely 'transferring' expert knowledge (largely based on risk) to passive patients. Information encompasses medical expertise but it also and necessarily includes the patient perspective, individual values and personal priorities. There will be inevitable variation in what clinicians and patients share. That is not problematic because no matter what the variables, effective clinicians will be consistently committed to adapting clinical evidence to individual circumstances in a way that is responsive, open and sensitive. For some patients, the results from large-scale studies and the reliability of such data will be their priority for discussion. For others, it may be the personality and style of the clinician or the timing of the procedure that preoccupies them when making a decision.

All patients should have an accurate sense of the proposed treatment, its aims, the principal risks and benefits and (often overlooked but essential if the patient is to understand that there is a choice) possible alternatives and the likely sequelae of not having the proposed treatment. However, this information is but a starting point in the consultation. In short, discussions about risks, percentages, probabilities and outcomes are necessary but not sufficient. An ethically astute clinician has a common goal with all patients: to share information in a way that is relevant, helpful and useful to individuals.

Endnotes

1. General Medical Council (2008). *Consent: Patients and Doctors Making Decisions Together*. London: General Medical Council.

2. For an excellent analysis of how a narrative-based approach to ethics might inform the seeking and obtaining of consent, see McMillan, J. and Gillett, G. (2002). Consent as empowerment. In K. W. M. Fulford, D. Dickenson and T. H. Murray, eds., *Healthcare Ethics and Human Values*. Oxford: Blackwell.

3. Beauchamp, T. L. and Childress, J. F. (2008). *Principles of Biomedical Ethics*. Oxford: Oxford University Press.

4. For a discussion of patient views about the value of information, see Manson, N. (2010). Why do patients want information if not to take part in decision making? *J Med Ethics* **36**, 834–7.

5. If Dr Hansen decides that she is going to give Mr Maitland less information than she might routinely do, it is good practice to record in the notes that she has made this choice with a brief explanation as to why; see Department of Health (2009). *Reference Guide on Consent to Examination and Treatment*, 2nd edn, para 21. London: HMSO.

6. General Medical Council (2008). *Consent Guidance: Patients and Doctors Making Decisions Together*, Part 2, paragraph 26. London: General Medical Council.

7. See also Department of Health (2009). *Reference Guide for Consent to Examination or Treatment*, 2nd edn, para 30. London: Department of Health, which stresses that ultimate responsibility remains with the clinician overseeing treatment.

8. See General Medical Council (2009). *The New Doctor*, para 6(c). London: General Medical Council.

9. See, for example, Read, K. and Shah, S. (2010). *Obtaining Informed Consent by Doctors in Training*. Cambridge, UK: East of England Deanery.

10. Wallace, L. M. (1986). Informed consent to elective surgery: the therapeutic value? *Soc Sci Med* **22**, 29–33; Teuten, B. and Taylor, D. (2001). 'Don't worry my good man – you won't understand our medical talk': consent to treatment today. *Br J Ophthalmol* **85**, 894–6; Akkad, A., Jackson, C., Kenyon, S., Dixon-Woods, M., Taub, N. and Habiba, M. (2004). Informed consent for elective and emergency surgery: questionnaire study. *Br J Obstet Gynaecol* **111**, 1133–8; Anderson, O. A. and Wearne, M. J. (2007). Informed consent for elective surgery: what is best practice? *J R Soc Med* **100**, 97–100; Ritchie, R. and Reynard, J. (2008). Consent for surgery: time for a standardised NHS consent checklist. *J R Soc Med* **101**, 48–49.

11. See both the original Department of Health Reference Guide on Consent (2001) and the revised, second edition, *Reference Guide for Consent to Examination and Treatment* (2009). London: HMSO.

12. For thoughtful accounts of what such an approach might mean in clinical practice, see Gilmartin, J. and Wright, K. (2008). Day surgery: patients felt abandoned during the preoperative wait. *J Clin Nurs* **17**, 2418–25; Lockey, J. and Ul-Hassan, M. (2009). Holistic approach to pre-operative assessment for cataract patients. *Br J Nurs* **18**, 326–7.

13. For an example of a study that considered the impact of nurse-led consent at a clinical centre, see Davis, M. (2005). Nurse-practitioner led consent in day case cataract surgery. *Nurs Times* **101**, 30–32. For an example of an audit reviewing nurse-led

consent, see Lockey, J. (2009). The provision of information for patients prior to cataract surgery. *Br J Nurs* **18**, 1207–11. For a review of what might constitute 'best practice' in day surgery, see Pearson, A., Richardson, M. and Cairns, M. (2004). 'Best practice' in day surgery units: a review of the evidence. *J Ambul Surg* **11**, 49–54.

14. See, for example, *North Glamorgan NHS Trust Protocol: Obtaining Written Consent for Elective Ophthalmic Procedures*, 2005.

15. *Making a Difference*. London: Department of Health (1999); *The NHS Plan*. London: Department of Health (2000); *Improving Endoscopy Services: Meeting the Challenges*. London: NHS Modernisation Agency (2004).

16. For a study exploring both the economic and clinical factors influencing professional practice, see Elliott, R. A., Payne, K., Moore, J. K. *et al.* (2003). Clinical and economic choices in anaesthesia for day surgery: a prospective randomised controlled trial. *Anaesthesia* **58**, 412–21.

17. Forster, A. J., LaBranche, R., McKim, R. *et al.* (2008). automated patient assessments after outpatient surgery using an interactive voice response system. *Am J Managed Care* **14**, 429–436; Law, T. T., Suen, D. T. K., Tam, Y. F. *et al.* (2009). Telephone pre-anaesthesia assessment for ambulatory breast surgery. *Hong Kong Med J* **15**, 179–82; Flanagan, J. (2009). Postoperative telephone calls: timing is everything. *AORN J* **90**, 41–51.

18. For examples of papers discussing the safety implications of nurse-led practice, see Gilmartin, J. and Wright, K. (2007). The nurse's role in day surgery: a literature review. *Int Nurs Rev* **54**, 183–90; Dartey, W., Borase, H., Organ, A., Evans, T. and Fox, R. (2010). Pre-operative assessment and consent for surgery: a role for the gynaecology nurse practitioner. *J Obstet Gynaecol* **30**, 166–70.

19. General Medical Council (2008). *Consent: Patients and Doctors Making Decisions Together*. London: General Medical Council.

20. As a civil action in the law of torts, claims have to be proven on the balance of probabilities.

21. For the interested, there is a wealth of literature and case law discussing the extent of that duty of care in particular or unusual circumstances, e.g. when travelling or in hospital car parks or when a clinician is off duty (the so-called 'Good Samaritan') cases.

22. *Bolam v. Friern Hospital Management Committee* [1957] 1 WLR 582.

23. Stacey, M. (1995). Medical accountability. In Hunt, G., ed., *Whistleblowing in the Health Service: Accountability, Law and Professional Practice*, pp. 35–49. London: Edward Arnold.

24. Samanta, A. and Samanta, J. (2003). Legal standard of care: a shift from the traditional *Bolam* test. *Clin Med* **3**, 443–6.

25. [1993] 4 Med LR 381.

26. Teff, H. (1998). The standard of care in medical negligence – moving on from *Bolam*? *Oxf J Le Stud* **18**, 473–84; Brazier, M. and Miola, J. (2000). Bye-bye *Bolam*: a medical

litigation revolution? *Med Law Rev* 8, 85–114; Khan, M. (2001). *Bolitho* – claimant's friend or enemy? *Med Law* 20, 483–91; McHale, J. (2002). Quality in healthcare: a role for the law? *Qual Saf Health Care* 11, 88–91.

27. It is possible that an action may lie in either the civil or criminal law (where the standard of proof is 'beyond reasonable doubt' rather than 'on the balance of probabilities').

28. Fox, R. (1957). Training for uncertainty. In Merton, R., Reader, G., Kendall, P., eds., *The Student Physician*. Cambridge, MA: Harvard University Press.

29. Fox, R. (2002). Medical uncertainty revisited. In G. Bendelow, M. Carpenter, C. Vautier and S. Williams, eds., *Gender, Health and Healing: The Public/Private Divide*. London: Routledge.

30. Hunter, K. (1996). 'Don't think zebras': uncertainty, interpretation and the place of paradox in clinical education. *Theor Med Bioeth* 17, 225–41.

31. It should not be assumed, however, that patients are insufficiently statistically sophisticated to understand the concepts underpinning evidence-based medicine. One of the authors recalls a complaint about the quality of consent sought and obtained by a patient who was, in his professional life, a world expert on mathematics and game theory.

32. A good introduction to this particular area is Melzer, D., Hogarth, S., Liddell, K. *et al.* (2008). Genetic tests for common diseases: new insights, old concerns. *BMJ* 336, 590–3.

33. See, for example, Cancer Backup Factsheet (2007) *DNA Analysis of BRCA1 and BRCA2 Genes.* Macmillan Cancer Support.

34. Parker, M. and Lucassen, A. (2003). Concern for families and individuals in clinical genetics. *J Med Ethics* 29, 70–3; Parker, M. and Lucassen, A. (2004). Genetic information: a joint account? *BMJ* 239 165–7.

35. Offit, K., Groeger, E., Turner, S., Wadsworth, E. A. and Weiser, M. A. (2004) The duty to warn a patient's family members about hereditary disease risks. *JAMA* 292, 1469–73.

Voluntariness: the freedom to choose

Introduction

For the seeking of consent to be a meaningful process, there must be a meaningful choice. In other words, consent must be voluntary. At first sight, this is a statement unlikely to surprise, and readers might be wondering why it warrants a chapter dedicated to voluntariness. However, agreeing to the importance of voluntariness in theory and ensuring its enactment in clinical practice are two distinct processes. It is also noticeable that in most of the literature relating to consent, attention to the subject of voluntariness is rare and, where it happens, discussions are usually focused on consent to participate in research. The vast majority of those reading this book will have little difficulty in nodding sagely in agreement with the statement that consent must be voluntary. Yet this chapter will argue that, in the daily practice of medicine, voluntariness can quickly be overlooked or compromised.

On the nature of coercion

Overt coercion in healthcare is rare. Most clinicians will not need persuading that coercion has no place in an effective therapeutic relationship. On closer examination, however, there are several factors that perhaps mean we should not dismiss coercion as an irrelevance without further thought.

Power

There is an inherent power imbalance between doctor and patient and between institution and individual. When a patient encounters a doctor, he or she does not do so as an equal. That is not to say that the healthcare professional believes patients to be inferior, but it is to acknowledge the stubbornly constant nature of power in the consultation. Social scientists were the first group to challenge the functionalist claims for the essential nature of medical work and to offer subsequent critiques that emphasized power.[1] The ways in which predominantly non-medical writers have described the medical profession range from apparently unquestioning endorsement of doctors as an altruistic group engaged in a noble art[2] to sneering, almost savage, critiques representing medics as a power-crazed, self-serving and protectionist elite.[3]

Michel Foucault offers one of the most interesting analyses of power in the medical profession, which remains influential. He occupies a distinct place in explorations of medical knowledge and the medical profession. His work is not concerned with the professionalization of medical practice but has a broader theoretical focus that depends on a dynamic, complex and fluid notion of power. The power of medical knowledge is asserted via the 'gaze'. From the 'gaze' come exclusive skills and a unique vocabulary distinguishing doctors as a professional group and thereby reinforcing status and collective power. In Foucault's world, power and knowledge in medicine are subtle, dispersed, sometimes chaotic, non-linear and multifactorial. Foucault offers an encompassing exploration of the language, vision, gestures, interactions and demeanour of medical practice, revealing the diverse, possibly infinite, nature of medical work. He moves the theoretical debate on from the barren polarity that can ensue from discussions of power: doctors are neither beneficent vessels for progress nor self-serving and deceiving masters of oppression. When doctors negotiate with patients in their daily practice, it involves power, expertise and their professional 'gaze'. Foucault argues that a doctor's power lies in its careful neutrality. The 'gaze' was powerful: it was powerful because a doctor in a formal location employed it.

It is important therefore to acknowledge that doctors are expert workers who wield considerable power, both in society and in consultations with individual patients, for, however much knowledge is accessible and shared rather than rarefied with patients as 'partners', there is an emotional dimension to the encounter that results in an unavoidable power imbalance. The patient has a problem and needs the doctor's advice, opinion or skills. The patient is dependent in a way that the doctor is not in the encounter. With power, comes discretion: the way in which the consultation is structured, the examination that is performed, the investigations offered and the treatment options discussed all remain largely the preserve of clinical discretion. The law too reinforces clinical discretion. Patients may express preferences and refuse treatment, but they are not entitled legally to demand treatment.

There is perhaps a moral distinction to be drawn between power and authority: power may be automatic and immutable, but authority has to be earned. The trick then is not to seek to eliminate power but to recognize it as inevitable, and to facilitate mutual trust and respect, thereby earning authority. A fundamental way in which mutual trust and respect are fostered and authority is earned is via the seeking of consent, which depends, in part, on the acknowledgement that the patient has a choice, which should be made as voluntarily as possible. Consider the scenario below – in what sense is the encounter and consent a voluntary process?

Mrs Eliza Marks, aged 32, is referred by her GP to the gynaecology outpatient clinic because she experiences severe symptoms of pre-menstrual syndrome (PMS), which have worsened since she had her first baby. Mrs Marks arrives at the clinic and is asked to change into a hospital gown. She is then weighed in the waiting room. When Mrs Marks enters the consultation room, she is asked to remove her underwear and wait on the examination couch for the consultant to arrive. Mr Scanlon, the consultant gynaecologist, arrives with his Registrar and a medical student. He greets Mrs Marks and asks her to assume the position for an internal pelvic examination, following which Mr Scanlon conducts a breast examination whilst explaining to the medical student what he is doing. Once the pelvic and breast examinations are completed, Mr Scanlon talks to Mrs Marks about her symptoms of PMS.

What Mr Scanlon and his colleagues take for granted as routine in the gynaecology outpatient clinic is likely to be novel, if not surprising and potentially disconcerting, for Mrs Marks. From the compulsory public weigh-in to the internal and breast examinations, it is a structure that does not pause to explain or invite Mrs Marks to express her own priorities or to ask questions. There may be sound clinical reasons for weighing and examining all patients, but the potential benefits and clinical rationale do not justify the absence of voluntariness that is embedded in the approach described in the scenario. Mr Scanlon, however well-intentioned and clinically outstanding he may be, has failed Mrs Marks by neither realizing the power imbalance that exists nor considering its impact on Mrs Marks. The consultation is driven by an approach that is professionally determined and not naturally patient-centred.

It would require only a small, but immeasurably significant, adjustment to the existing arrangements to redress the balance and allow Mrs Marks meaningful choice. Firstly, she should be advised in advance of the appointment of the likely process she will experience when she comes to the clinic. If all patients are routinely weighed, asked to put on gowns and given internal and breast examinations irrespective of the presenting symptoms, that should be explained. As part of that explanation, Mrs Marks should understand that she is able to ask questions about why such an approach is considered desirable and what the implications might be if she were to refuse any part of the 'routine'. Mrs Marks should also understand that she may see more than one member of clinical staff and that the team may include students. Just like the 'routine' weighing, gowning and examinations, she should be able to choose whether she wishes to have a student participate in her care. It is not sufficient to assume that, because Mrs Marks has walked through the hospital doors, she has willingly acceded to whatever follows. Merely being referred by a GP and entering the monolithic system of the UK National Health Service (NHS) does not preclude patients from choosing or refusing care at each stage.

Voluntariness relies on professionals to make genuine efforts to listen to patients, attending to both verbal and non-verbal cues. The worries of patients can be surprising and may be unanticipated by busy clinicians for whom the consultation is 'routine'. A few moments spent in open and non-defensive discussion is likely to be time well spent, leading to trust, an effective therapeutic alliance and ultimately improved care and outcomes for patient and professional alike.

Systemic coercion

Healthcare takes place in a system where multiple variables influence priorities and practice. The ways in which the system of healthcare fosters coercion are considerable and warrant attention.

Firstly, there are the ways in which doctors structure their practice. Consider, for example, the ward round: a process whereby the patient sits passively while a number of people discuss him or her before making decisions and moving on. Whilst there is variance in the ways in which individual clinicians conduct their ward rounds (with some even abandoning the concept completely), it remains the case that most clinical teams have something like a ward round where care is reviewed at the bedside with a group of staff. Whatever options are discussed during the ward round, it is likely to compromise the patient's ability to choose freely and participate in his or her care.

Consider the scenario below.

A large ward round comprising a dozen people reaches the bed of Mr Birch, a patient who was admitted for investigations following an unexplained 'collapse'. The consultant, Dr Tully, proposes that the patient should have an echocardiogram, an exercise stress test and begin treatment for hypertension. Dr Tully does not explain his decision to Mr Birch. Later, Mr Birch calls the nursing staff in some distress and tells them that he will not go down for investigations or take any medication because he has no idea what is going on.

The situation described in the scenario above is so common that it is considered by many not only to be the norm but a necessary medical tradition: the ward round. The mere format of the ward round makes a nonsense of much ethical teaching and advice. Confidentiality, privacy and dignity are difficult to preserve in a standard ward round. Even the most assiduous curtain puller and blanket rearranger will struggle to ensure that the precepts of respect for patient autonomy, shared decision-making and confidential disclosure of information are enacted in a ward round. Merely because something is done a particular way in most places does not render it right. It is difficult to maintain ethical practice in an imperfect system.

Mr Birch is refusing treatment that is in his best interests because he does not feel he has been involved in his care, still less given a choice about what is to happen. To proceed under such circumstances would not only be unethical, it would be an assault.

Secondly, this vignette reveals what lies beneath and can become lost in formulaic approaches to consent, namely the therapeutic relationship and trust between patient and clinician that has indubitably been compromised. The diminution of trust is a significant ethical challenge with potentially serious consequences for both the patient and the clinical team. It is essential that someone, ideally Dr Tully, rectifies matters by apologizing, explaining what is happening and seeking Mr Birch's consent to proceed. He has to be promoted from his non-speaking role as played out in the ward round to a fully involved participant in his care who understands that investigations and treatment are options to be explored, not commands to be executed.

A further area where systemic factors can affect voluntariness is where there are conditions placed on patient choice, often for very good reasons. The freedom to consent, as has already been noted, is not equivalent to a freedom to demand or make unfettered requests. However, the negotiation of what might be called the 'terms and conditions' of consent is interesting. For example, consider the many situations in which a patient's treatment is contingent upon factors that are outwith the strict boundaries of medical intervention but are nonetheless significant such as the requirement that a patient undergoing a cataract operation or an endoscopy should be accompanied by a third party to provide safe transport home. Clearly, the professionals caring for patients have a responsibility to ensure that patients are able to go home without putting themselves or others at avoidable risk, but the extent to which discussion of these sorts of mandatory issues are included in the consent process and the effect on the notion of voluntariness warrants thought and attention.

Moving towards the more medical terrain, consider the negotiation of risk in clinical practice and the implications for seeking and obtaining consent. Clinicians are used to the parts that make up the whole of the treatment, but patients are not. Many readers will be familiar with the patient who willingly agrees to the measurement of arterial blood gas on the first occasion but becomes markedly more reluctant to undergo the procedure again when they have experienced how painful it can be. Clearly, there are many situations, perhaps the majority of situations, where a host of interventions comprise a package of effective treatment or care. To treat appropriately, the blood gas measurement is essential, but to the patient it is a painful and curious version of the more tolerable venous 'blood test' that is more commonly encountered. The majority will, of course, agree to the transient discomfort of the procedure once it is explained that it is integral to making a reliable diagnosis and providing effective treatment. The point of including it in this discussion of consent is to highlight that much which is taken for granted by professionals may be seen as strange and unwelcome. It is the role of the clinician to help the patient navigate the system and to facilitate an appreciation of healthcare as a process within a system.

Careful attention to consent, and in particular that which is assumed as the clinical default, is an essential and integral part of building trust and developing an effective therapeutic alliance with shared, rather than competing, goals.

A second example of how the system can compromise voluntariness on the part of the patient involves elective surgery: who should decide whether a patient with a cold or other mild upper respiratory tract infection is sufficiently well to be anaesthetized for a long-awaited and much-needed surgery? Clearly, there are sound clinical reasons for wishing patients to be as well as possible prior to receiving an anaesthetic and undergoing surgery, but to what extent is the risk negotiable? If a patient understands that there is a risk of proceeding with surgery whilst he or she has a cold, is it within his or her gift to decide whether that is a risk he or she wishes to take? Or is it a matter for the anaesthetist and surgeon (we shall not, at this point, be distracted by professional differences in anaesthetic and surgical opinion)?

For many, there is a clear delineation between what are considered clinical matters of professional judgement that should be determined by doctors and that which is a personal, social or emotional matter that should properly be for the patient to decide. Yet there is inherent morality in determining the boundaries between patient and professional and marking out the terrain over which each party rules. The process of agreeing who decides what, when and how reflects ethical assumptions about the value of knowledge and expertise, notions of service and ownership of risk. The misleadingly simple, or at least misleadingly operationalized, approach to consent is revealed to be but the tip of an ethical iceberg with assumptions about epistemology, status and conflicts of interest lurking darkly beneath. Fortunately, most consultations do not require complex negotiation between patient and clinician, and understandably the shared aim of a good outcome is sufficient to ensure that the iceberg can be deftly avoided. However, it is important to know that the iceberg is there and to have some insight into what lies beneath. It may not be common, but at some stage most clinicians will encounter a situation where a patient is seeking something that comes with unwelcome conditions or disagrees about the sorts of risk he or she is willing to take.

Consider and compare the scenarios below.

Mr Jack Lyons is 22 years old. He has recently been admitted to the general adult psychiatric ward as a voluntary patient. Dr Gupta, the consultant psychiatrist, would like to begin treatment with lithium. Dr Gupta describes why she believes lithium will be helpful for Jack, and explains that he will have to have regular blood tests to ensure that the dose is correct. Mr Lyons tells Dr Gupta that he does not object to taking lithium if she thinks it is the best treatment for him, but he does not want to have regular blood tests.

Mrs Virginia Cairns is 77 years old and a widow who lives alone. She has come in for a partial knee replacement. Dr Martin, the anaesthetist, visits Mrs Cairns on the morning of the operation. As Dr Martin takes a history, it becomes clear that Mrs Cairns has a mild cold but is otherwise well. Dr Martin explains that she prefers not to anaesthetize patients when they are unwell. Mrs Cairns tearfully replies, *'It is only a slight cold. I must get this operation done today. I have organized everything: my younger sister and daughter have arranged to come and stay to help me when I am discharged and it is all planned – trains are booked and my daughter has taken time off work. I have been waiting a long time and I am in so much pain.'*

In the scenarios above, both patients have encountered conditions to the treatment that is indicated and that which they are willing, even eager, to receive. It is not surprising that such situations occur: people approach doctors because they are seeking advice and professional guidance. Patients are frequently unaware of the indications for, and limitations to, treatment. Even a well-informed person who has researched his or her symptoms and condition is unlikely to appreciate, in depth, when, why and how care is provided. Consent is not about pitching professional against patient. Consent should foster and enhance the therapeutic relationship, not undermine it by setting one party's list of demands against another's. Ultimately, in both situations there is work to be done in explaining, listening and sharing the questions that arise for Mr Lyons and Mrs Cairns.

Let us consider Mr Lyons first: he can only safely receive the treatment he seeks by acceding to regular blood tests; to prescribe without him understanding that blood testing is an integral part of treatment with lithium would be dangerous and professionally unacceptable. Whilst Mr Lyons might perceive the requirement for blood testing as a separate and burdensome adjunct to treatment, that perception is a misunderstanding and warrants discussion by Dr Gupta. It is her task not to coerce Mr Lyons into agreeing that he will present for regular blood tests but to explain why the blood tests are essential for the safe and effective prescription of lithium. It is not a matter of professional power trumping patient freedom but rather a reflection of what it is to practise in a way that is meaningfully patient-centred and responsive. It requires Dr Gupta to remember what it is like not to know and to imagine what it is to be a frightened and vulnerable young man with a newly diagnosed psychiatric condition. It is an ethical issue that can only properly be addressed by empathy, patience and a sincere commitment to involving Mr Lyons in his care. It is a scenario that demonstrates why the approach of the individual clinician is crucial in seeking consent and why the process of obtaining consent is much more nuanced and complex than that which can be captured on a standard form.

The scenario involving Mrs Cairns and her suitability for surgery might prompt a less uniform response amongst clinicians than that of Mr Lyons and treatment with lithium. Mild upper respiratory viral infections are common, particularly in winter, and patients who present for surgery will often have a 'slight cold'. Most people have learned (often from doctors) that colds are insignificant inconveniences and not something to cause medical concern. Indeed, many patients will have had experience of a GP advising that a viral infection is not medically serious, does not warrant treatment beyond simple, over-the-counter symptomatic management and is likely to be self-limiting. Therefore, it is unsurprising that many people will disregard minor viral symptoms and present for surgery. It is understandable that Mrs Cairns is both surprised and upset that her 'cold' might prevent her from having her long-awaited operation, particularly given the meticulous planning that has gone in to making arrangements to care for her after surgery. Dr Martin, like Dr Gupta, has to explain why there is a relationship between even a minor 'cold' and the decision to anaesthetize a patient.

However, unlike the scenario involving Dr Gupta, it is less clear what the risks might be and, perhaps more interestingly, whose risks they are to accept or reject. Anaesthetists are likely to have different thresholds for determining when a patient is too unwell to receive an anaesthetic. In people who are chronically ill, there is no choice but to proceed with an anaesthetic and the risks have to be integrated into the process of giving information and seeking consent. However, where patients like Mrs Cairns become riskier anaesthetic propositions because of self-limiting and minor illness, there are two questions to consider: (i) what is the risk (assuming it is knowable and even then acknowledging the limitations of generalizing from large-scale studies to specific individuals), and (ii) if Mrs Cairns is prepared to take that risk, should that be sufficient for Dr Martin to agree to anaesthetize her or does it remain within Dr Martin's gift to refuse to anaesthetize a patient whom she believes to be at increased risk?

As has already been noted, ethically, the principle of patient autonomy in Western ethics has been argued by some to be pre-eminent. All those who have capacity have the right of self-determination and their choices should be respected. Does this ethical model in which autonomy is the predominant principle translate into unfettered choice in all healthcare encounters? It is argued that this is not the case because such a conclusion depends on a simplistic misinterpretation of, and response to, the concept of autonomy, both personal and professional.

The way in which the ethical question or 'problem' is understood and phrased is integral to the ensuing analysis and eventual conclusions. Therefore, careful attention should be paid to the 'naming' of an ethical problem. In this situation, it is not whether a patient's autonomy takes priority over a doctor's professional autonomy that is the question, but how autonomy can be facilitated, developed, maximized and shared by Mrs Cairns and Dr Martin. As such, and like the discussion of Mr Maitland and Dr Hansen in Chapter 3, 'autonomy' (personal or professional) is not something to be fought over but a common aim of clinician and patient in which sharing contrasting, or even conflicting, perspectives allows and demands dialogue, discussion and decision-making based on mutual respect and increased understanding.

Given the relative positions of clinician and patient in the consultation that were discussed earlier in this chapter, what does it mean for Dr Martin to foster patient autonomy? Perhaps it means rejecting notions of autonomy that are constructed in an artificially binary way, as 'all-or-nothing' choices. Meaningful choices cannot be made in a moral and social vacuum. Just as cultural relativism recognizes and explores the social, temporal and geographical determinants that result in varied constructions of moral principles, so too ethicists who argue for the pre-eminence of patient autonomy should reflect on the social and cultural context in which autonomy is not only constructed but can be developed and respected. Frequently, in healthcare, this is an imperceptible daily negotiation in which compromise is possible, but occasionally a patient's choice is in direct opposition to a doctor's choice. In such circumstances, it is unhelpful and unethical for the conflict between doctor and patient preference to become a battle: such an approach is likely to result in dissatisfaction for both parties. Rather, this is the time to explore why there are apparent irreconcilable differences between patient and doctor perspectives and return to perhaps the primary duty of the clinician: to serve the patient's interests in a professional, altruistic and disinterested way.

In order to do this, an exchange of information about why there is a difference between the doctor's and patient's perception of whether and how an upper respiratory tract infection contributes to the common goal of 'best interests' is required. Dr Martin may feel that she should not anaesthetize Mrs Cairns for reasons of clinical judgement, policy, evidence, medico-legal concerns or simply intuition. Even if complications and poor outcomes are rare, does comparative infrequency justify Dr Martin acting in a way that is contrary to her professional judgement and places patient autonomy above all else?

In contrast, Mrs Cairns has reasons for wishing to proceed that extend well beyond the purely clinical. For Mrs Cairns, the risks of proceeding with surgery are but one element in a complex array of social, emotional and practical considerations, and she may be disconcerted by what she perceives as the reframing of a management plan that has been made with a clinical team that she trusts. To represent the complexity of variables that influence both professional and patient responses to risk as a competition between doctor and patient choice is simplistic, unhelpful and ultimately counter-therapeutic.

The notion that professional autonomy is subservient to patient autonomy on every occasion is to render clinicians to the status of patient-directed technicians and diminishes the knowledge, skills and therapeutic value of medical training (although it might equally be argued that requiring absolute adherence to formalized professional guidelines likewise diminishes professional expertise). Patient autonomy does not mean that a patient is able to determine absolutely what she would like without reference to professional judgement. Of course, it does not follow that patient autonomy, if not respected absolutely, is inevitably sacrificed at the altar of paternalistic medical authority. Rather, it reflects that autonomy is less about a competition in which patient and professional preferences jostle for philosophical priority but depends on an ethos of respect, equality, trust and shared enterprise in which conflicting interests are balanced, and are not either completely dominant or eliminated entirely.

Once autonomy is reinterpreted for both Dr Martin and Mrs Cairns as a common process with the shared aim of improving health, the issue of which party's preference should 'trump' the other party's preference in the consultation becomes redundant. The ethical issue is not whether Mrs Cairns can demand that surgery goes ahead, but whether Dr Martin can create a non-judgemental atmosphere in which Mrs Cairns feels she can explain her preference and Dr Martin can enhance her autonomy by explaining why her preference is ill-advised. From the sharing of information comes awareness and challenging of assumptions and the 'problem' can be reframed: no longer is it a question of frustration at conflicting professional and personal wishes but a process of understanding that the 'wishes' of both doctor and patient are socially, psychologically and culturally located. It is not about either party 'defending' their position but exploring, and explaining, the differences in their respective perspectives. To do so is to create, perpetuate and respect autonomy in a far more meaningful and ethically sustainable way than to merely accede to, or refuse, patient 'demands'. The exchange of perspective is, it is argued, the ultimate ethical tool in seeking and obtaining consent. Without it, discussions of autonomy are meaningless and the risks to the therapeutic relationship considerable.

Another area in which systemic coercion can occur is opportunistic screening and interventions, which are increasingly being encouraged by healthcare policy as clinicians are exhorted to seize the moment and to use consultations to undertake activities that may be unrelated to whatever the patient originally wished to discuss. The place in which this is most prevalent is general practice. As the Quality and Outcomes Framework used in the UK became part of practice, so more GPs were encouraged to measure blood pressure and discuss smoking should the opportunity arise. It used to be the case that patients would commonly utter the words, '*While I'm here, Doctor ...*' Now, it is equally likely that the doctor will be saying '*While you're here ...*' to the patients. In some ways, the opportunistic screening of blood pressure is a laudable aim, but there are ethical difficulties. Simply put, such an approach to medicine inevitably compromises voluntariness to some extent because it is not what the patient was seeking from the consultation. It may well be that an opportunistic measurement of a person's blood pressure reveals that treatment is indicated, but outcomes are far from the entire ethical story when it comes to consent;

no matter how positive the outcome, even if patients are saved from death, to act without an individual's consent is to breach the fundamentals of ethical practice.

Once a patient agrees to undergo most 'routine' screening, there is a potential chain of further investigations and perhaps a life-time of treatment. Some types of screening can lead to an invasive test; in what sense is an individual's choice to undergo the invasive test 'free'? One way to think ethically about such situations is to consider the concept of 'contingent autonomy', i.e. if a person is properly counselled when deciding whether or not to have screening, he or she will be encouraged to consider what choices he or she would prefer to make if further investigations and/or treatment are indicated. Even if someone decides that he or she does not wish to pursue screening, that decision should be informed by a dialogue with clinicians that enable the patient to leave feeling more informed about the options. So-called 'contingent autonomy' emphasizes the importance of effective pre-screening consultations whilst not, of course, removing the need for a person to give valid consent to any future treatment.

External drivers and influences on practice such as the Quality and Outcomes Framework and performance indicators require clinicians to think harder than ever about the nature of voluntariness in relation to consent. Irrespective of guidelines, protocols, reminders on the computer screen or targets, doctors have to be alert to, and facilitate, choice. It is even more important where potential conflicts of interest exist. For example, the GP who meets the targets set by the Quality and Outcomes Framework will be rewarded financially for doing so. Likewise, the hospital consultant who enrols patients to a trial will benefit. Measuring outcomes and categorizing care may be valued and valuable, but it is a potential distraction from ensuring that patients are aware of the range of choices available to them and might, if not well managed, vitiate the voluntariness of consent.

Guidelines, evidence-based medicine and preventative measures have transformed healthcare in the last 20 years. Much of what has been achieved is positive: a more rigorous approach to practice, continuing professional development and improved patient care as a result of timely interventions. However, it remains the case that healthcare, even optimal, effective and externally endorsed healthcare, is a choice. Patients rely on their doctors to help them make those choices and the first step is to explain that there are choices to be made. From the facilitation of choice comes openness, trust and mutual understanding – qualities that cannot be measured by outcome frameworks or performance indicators but which are immeasurably valuable in the practice of medicine.

Relatives, friends and others

Most doctors will have experience of the significance of third parties in their practice. Relatives and friends can be extremely helpful. Clinicians may become used to seeing family members visiting a patient on a ward or accompanying a patient to clinic. Third parties may reassure the patient, advocate his or her interests and act as an effective supporter. However, third parties, sometimes even those who are absent entirely, can influence patient choice in a way that has an effect on the voluntariness of consent.

The starting point for consent to all healthcare investigations and treatment is that it is a decision made by an individual (assuming he or she has capacity). It is a matter of personal choice, and those choices should be made without the influence or even coercion of others, however well intentioned. Yet one only has to reflect on the ways in which human beings interact with others to realize that the notion of a person as a separate entity who neither considers nor responds to those around him or her is artificial and potentially unhelpful. We are all, to a greater or lesser extent, the product of influence. Our development is shaped by parents and teachers, our growing independence is fostered by powerful comparisons and relationships with our peers and, as adults, most of us choose to live with others and form our own social units and families. Everyone is, to some degree, the product of the relationships we have experienced and formed. Much of our lives is spent learning to consider the feelings and wishes of others, being considerate in our choices and looking out for the interests of those whom we love. In many ways, the ethical premise that individuals exist like self-contained atoms making a series of discrete choices in life unencumbered by the needs, preferences and priorities of others is empirically unrealistic and potentially unhelpful.

The emphasis on individual choice and independence as an expression of personal autonomy has been challenged by many writers in the field of bioethics. George Agich in his work on long-term care and the older person[4] has suggested that 'actual autonomy' for those who have chronic disease is interdependent, interactionist and social. It is only by attending to the empirical experience of relationships and emotions, he argues, that clinicians can understand what it means to support people in making decisions about healthcare. For many, choices, especially significant choices that involve health and illness, will always be an endeavour to be shared with those close to them and caring for them.

Onora O'Neill also considered the notion of individual autonomy in her Reith Lectures and subsequent writing.[5] Although her focus has tended to be more on the relationship between the professional and the patient than on family relationships, she too highlights the importance of trust, loyalties and the effects on others in making moral decisions, and argues that all of these variables are potentially compromised if individualism becomes the sole preoccupation. It is an argument that is likely to lead to an approach that is both more familiar (and the choice of adjective may itself be revealing) and comfortable to many clinicians whereby individual patients involve family members, partners, friends and significant others.

Indeed, most clinicians will know that it is not just those who are present who are frequently invoked in the consultation: calls may be made to those living far away, deceased parents are remembered when people are faced with their own mortality, beloved children and grandchildren are invoked as reasons to accept treatment, and so on. When doctor and patient sit together in clinics and surgeries, they are joined, metaphorically at least, by a cast of characters who inevitably inform that dyadic interaction. To acknowledge the influence of others therefore is unavoidable and ethically essential. That is not to say that patients should be subject to duress or undue pressure from others, but it is to suggest that unless a clinician explores what influences a patient is bringing to his or her choices, autonomy and therefore consent is likely to be less than it could or should be.

As part of the process of exploring the relationships that are significant to an individual patient, at some stage a clinician will encounter relatives who may appear to be unduly dominant and/or not to be acting in a patient's best interests. Whilst such a realization may be discomforting, it is significant ethically, and merely by realizing what influences there are on a person's choices, the likelihood of supporting the patient more effectively is enhanced. It is also worth reflecting on what underpins the discomfort that such a situation may cause because it elucidates further the basis on which significant others are generally accepted to have a role in another's healthcare decisions, namely that there is a bond of love and affection from which is born a commitment to promote the patient's welfare. Where a relative or third party appears to be acting in a way that compromises or undermines the patient's best interests, a fundamental moral assumption is challenged, which results in the sinking feeling that may be familiar to many clinicians. What then might the response be when a clinician realizes that his or her patient is subject to pressure from others who may not prioritize the patient's best interests?

Where someone is acting in a way that seems to subsume or disregard the interests of the patient, the clinician has a duty to respond by expressing concerns and explaining why he or she is keen to hear from the patient. As with much of ethics, it is a duty that is easier to accede to in the abstract than in reality. However, if one believes that a patient has capacity to make a choice, it is the clinician's role to ensure that, as far as possible, the patient is able to make that choice. Asking to see a patient alone or deliberately creating space to see the patient alone if possible is a practical first step. Naturally, even when individuals are seen alone, the extent of third-party influence can still loom large in the consultation, but it is easier to have a conversation where the clinician can neutrally, but explicitly, 'name' his or her concerns that the patient should be able to freely discuss the options, consider his or her priorities and make a settled choice without undue attention to the perspectives of other people. Where it is not possible to see a patient alone, it may be that the clinician has to act more deliberately as the patient's advocate and draw on the therapeutic alliance to represent the patient's interests and explain why a relative's perspective may be problematic or even harmful. It is important to remember, however, that many relatives, just like patients, are afraid of what is unknown. For example, the relative who appears to be insisting on continued treatment that is considered aggressive or inappropriate by the clinical team may be fearful of the patient being 'abandoned' and misunderstand that the withdrawal of active treatment is not equivalent to 'no care'. Similarly, wishes expressed as part of decision-making at the end of life may be indicative of lack of knowledge about what might constitute 'a good death'.

In a minority of cases, relatives may be flouting a patient's best interests to such a degree that more formal action is required. For example, even where a patient has nominated a proxy via the Lasting Power of Attorney provisions, that power to make decisions on another's behalf is limited to the extent to which the proxy acts in a person's best interests. Likewise, in the case of children, those with parental responsibility are empowered to make choices only so far as they are acting in the child's best interests. The freedom of third parties to shape care is not unfettered, and sometimes the ethical doctor will have to be the one who engages in fettering the involvement of others.

There are some situations where, as well as third parties acting on behalf of patients, there is also a dependency on the hierarchy of relationships. In seeking consent for organ donation where there is no evidence of a patient's preferences, the law requires that consent is sought from someone with whom the potential donor was in an established relationship. In England and Wales, the Human Tissue Act 2004 uses the term 'qualifying relative'. The list of potential parties who can be approached is wide and includes parents, spouses, partners,[6] siblings, grandparents, nieces, nephews, grandchildren and long-standing friends. Step-parents and half-siblings can also be 'qualifying relatives'. 'Qualifying relatives' are ranked under the Human Tissue Act 2004 in the following order:

- Spouse or partner
- Parent or child
- Sibling
- Grandparent or grandchild
- Niece or nephew
- Step-parent
- Half-sibling
- Friend of longstanding

Consent for organ donation should be sought from the highest-ranking relative. Where there is more than one person who is an equally ranking relative, for example, parents or siblings, the consent of one person will suffice. The law provides that, even if a person is of the highest rank to make a decision about donation on behalf of a deceased patient, that person is entitled to opt out of the decision-making process either because of preference or because he or she is unable to participate due to, for example, incapacity. The code of practice that accompanies the Human Tissue Act 2004 emphasizes that seeking consent in relation to organ donation is a process and requires that clinicians check that consent is continuing right up until the point at which donation is scheduled to begin. Where relatives disagree about organ donation, the law requires clinicians to consider whether the distress caused by proceeding with donation in the face of disagreement can justify going ahead with organ donation. Unfortunately, where the wishes of the potential donor are unknown, evidence suggests that approximately 40% of qualifying relatives will not consent to organ donation.[7]

Legal limits to voluntariness

The law provides for some limited circumstances in which compulsion rather than voluntary consent is acceptable, including admission and treatment under the Mental Health Acts 1983 and 2007, deprivation of liberty orders under the Mental Capacity Act 2005, compulsory examination and detention under the Public Health (Control of Disease) Act 1984 (as amended) and referrals to the Court of Protection. In such situations, the ethico-legal rationale for forgoing the voluntariness that is otherwise considered to be fundamental to consent is that the patient's best interests and/or those of society at large warrant compulsion. Irrespective of the situation, voluntary admission and treatment remains the preferred model. Merely because a power to compel a patient exists, it does not mean it should become the default option.

Public health, compulsion and consent

Consider the scenario below.

> Miss Lumanda, aged 26, presents at the accident and emergency department because she has been 'coughing and sweating' for several weeks. Miss Lumanda is living in a hostel. Having taken a history and examined Miss Lumanda, tuberculosis is part of the differential diagnosis. Investigations and X-rays confirm that Miss Lumanda has tuberculosis, but she is reluctant to be admitted.

The traditional model in medical ethics and law is based on the encounter between an individual clinician and patient. In such a model, all ethico-legal duties, rights and dilemmas are understood as flowing from this dyadic (and often one-off) encounter. However, there is increasing attention being paid to the population perspective and the ethico-legal issues that arise thereof. The problems posed by communicable diseases are increasingly significant. Adherence and concordance on the part of patients who are diagnosed with tuberculosis are vital if relapse and the development of drug-resistant disease are to be avoided.

What powers do, and should, doctors have in respect of patients who are smear-positive and are, at best, erratic about complying with treatment regimes? Should practitioners have the power to detain compulsorily such patients? The moral rationale for compulsory detention is generally said to be the utilitarian argument that the effect on individual autonomy of compulsory detention is a smaller loss than the potential damage such an individual can cause to society if he or she is not detained. However, given that patients with tuberculosis are frequently (but not necessarily) marginalized within society, it has been suggested that such measures are indicative of discrimination. Richard Coker[8] has argued that ethical practice demands that clinically informed assessment of risk and the exploration of less restrictive alternative approaches to adherence must precede any move towards compulsion. The Public Health (Control of Disease) Act 1984, and specifically sections 37 and 38, which, on the authority of a Magistrate (Justice of the Peace), permitted the removal and detention of patients to prevent infection, have been the subject of both academic debate and an extensive consultation on reform[9] leading to revised powers of compulsion under the Health and Social Care Act 2008.[10]

The priority when working with Miss Lumanda is to ensure that she is aware of her diagnosis and receives optimal treatment. Developing a trusting therapeutic relationship is likely to go further than cajoling, admonishing or even threatening her with compulsory powers. Her legitimate concerns about her housing must not be ignored, and the discussion should be informed by resources that describe the support available to people who are at risk of unlawful eviction. Services may be available that will ease the burden of treatment for Miss Lumanda, particularly costs relating to transport, temporary housing and prescription charges. Demonstrating both an understanding of stigma, empathy for Miss Lumanda's fear regarding her hostel place and knowledge of the resources available to minimize the impact of diagnosis and treatment make it more likely that the patient will understand rather than fear treatment. The complexities of compulsion should not dominate. The aim is to respond as required by law while developing a relationship of trust with a vulnerable woman who is frightened that she will be further marginalized. Such a relationship is likely to be the foundation for an effective treatment programme and will protect both Miss Lumanda's individual interests and those of the wider community.

Mental health, compulsion and consent

It is important to stress that many patients being treated for psychiatric illness have capacity to make choices about healthcare. Voluntariness in the form of freely given consent based on an open exchange of information between patient and doctor is both the ethical ideal and the clinical reality in many situations. However, there are some circumstances where mental illness will compromise an individual's ability to make his or her own decisions. In such circumstances, specific legislation curtails the requirement of voluntarily given consent and enables treatment without consent on the basis that the patient is a risk to themselves and/or to others.

Those who have or are suspected of having a mental disorder may be detained for assessment and treatment in England and Wales under the Mental Health Act 2007 (which amended the 1983 statute also called the Mental Health Act). There is one definition of a mental disorder for the purposes of the law, which is a significant development from the somewhat confused and confusing categories that were set out in the 1983 legislation. Notably, one of the most common and growing areas of mental disorder, namely addiction to and dependence on drugs and/or alcohol, is excluded from the definition of mental disorder under the statute. The rationale for the exclusion is interesting. For treatment of addiction and dependence to be successful, it is commonly thought to be a requirement that the subject be willing to participate. In other words, irrespective of risk to themselves or others, addiction and dependence are an area of illness that can be treated only where there is voluntariness on the part of the patient, who must make a free choice to seek and participate in treatment. Where addiction or dependence co-exists with another mental disorder (dual diagnosis), compulsory powers may be used to detain a person under the Mental Health Act, but where the sole concern is addiction or dependence, the compulsory powers under the Mental Health legislation cannot be used.

Appropriate medical treatment should be available to those who are admitted under the Mental Health Act. In addition to assessment and treatment in hospital, the legislation now provides for compulsory treatment and limits to voluntariness beyond the psychiatric ward or hospital in the form of Supervised Community Treatment Orders. Such orders consist of supervised community treatment after a period of detention in hospital. The law is tightly defined with multiple checks and limitations, which are essential given the ethical implications of detaining and treating someone against his or her will.

Even where a detained patient may lawfully be given psychiatric treatment compulsorily and therefore the usual requirement of voluntariness is potentially unnecessary, efforts should be made to obtain consent, if possible. Compulsory assessment and treatment under the Mental Health Act are limited to mental disorders. For physical illness, a person's capacity should be assessed using the Mental Capacity Act 2005, as discussed in Chapter 2. If someone has capacity, consent should be obtained to treat for anything other than the mental disorder as if seeking to treat anyone without a mental disorder. If someone lacks capacity because of the severity of their psychiatric illness or by virtue of any other inhibiting factor that compromises capacity, treatment for physical symptoms should be given on the basis of best interests or with reference to a proxy or advance decision if applicable. If treatment can wait, without seriously compromising a person's interests, consent should be sought when a person once more has capacity.

The key message is that, whilst there are circumstances where the law allows for compulsory treatment of a mental disorder, the extent of that permission is strictly defined and limited.

Mental capacity, deprivation of liberty and consent

An area where voluntariness is potentially limited and that is attracting increasing attention is the use of Deprivation of Liberty orders under the Mental Capacity Act 2005. Deprivation of Liberty orders were included in the Mental Capacity Act following the high profile case of *HL v. UK* [11] (often known as 'the *Bournewood* case') in which the European Court of Human Rights decided that people who lacked capacity and were detained for treatment or care on a voluntary basis, such as those with learning disabilities or autism, were entitled to formal legal protection. As a result, the Mental Capacity Act 2005 includes Safeguards that apply when a Deprivation of Liberty order is in place that are intended to protect an individual who lacks capacity and has been detained for care in his or her best interests. The Safeguards and Code of Practice set out by the Mental Capacity Act provide the legal framework for decisions where the voluntary element of consent can be overridden and the Court of Protection provides oversight of the enactment of the law. However, the numbers of Deprivation of Liberty orders [12] and some individual stories [13] as reported in the media have raised questions about their use and the effectiveness or otherwise of the Safeguards. In common with compulsory admission and treatment under the Mental Health Act, a Deprivation of Liberty order is a last resort and it should be clear why the interests of the patient justify compulsory detention. [14]

Voluntariness: concluding thoughts

This chapter has argued that voluntariness is a comparatively underconsidered aspect of consent that warrants greater attention from ethicists and clinicians alike. To be aware of the variables that shape clinical relationships, alert to the respective roles and priorities of each party, questioning of professional assumptions and conscious of the effect of systemic factors that potentially limit or remove patient choice is to be an ethical practitioner. Consent, and its voluntary deliverance, becomes a conduit for building trust, communicating honestly and fostering respect. The clinician and the patient embark on a moral enterprise that can never be captured in a hastily signed consent form and that often exists in spite of, rather than because of, systemic approaches to patient care.

Endnotes

1. Eliot Freidson was particularly influential in making a connection between power and professional knowledge, and did so with unprecedented persistence. Freidson has developed his influential ideas about the medical profession over 40 years.

2. Jacob, J. M. (1999). *Doctors and Rules: a Sociology of Professional Values*. London: Routledge.

3. Millman, M. (1977). *The Unkindest Cut: Life in the Backrooms of Medicine*. New Haven: Yale University Press.

4. Agich, G. (1993). *Autonomy and Long-term Care*. Oxford: Oxford University Press; Agich, G. (2003). *Dependence and Autonomy in Old Age: an Ethical Framework for Long-term Care*. Oxford: Oxford University Press; Agich, G. (2004). Seeking the everyday meaning of autonomy in neurological disorders. *Philos Psychiatr Psychol* 11, 295–8.

5. O'Neill, O. (2003). *Autonomy and Trust in Bioethics*. Cambridge: Cambridge University Press; O'Neill, O. (2003). Some limits of informed consent. *J Med Ethics* 29, 1–5.

6. Including civil partners by virtue of a legal order under the Civil Partnership Act 2004.

7. British Medical Association (2007). *Presumed Consent for Organ Donation*. London: British Medical Association. The low levels of organ donation relative to other European countries and the limited numbers of people on the NHS Donor Register have led to the current debate about presumed consent in which variations on an 'opt-out' system to replace the current 'opt-in' system have been proposed. However, the government-commissioned independent report from the Organ Donation Taskforce rejected a system predicated on 'presumed consent' from which people would opt out; see Department of Health (2008). *The Potential Impact of an Opt-Out System of Organ Donation in the United Kingdom: an Independent Report from the Organ Donation Taskforce*. London: Department of Health.

8. Coker, R. (2000). Tuberculosis, non-compliance and detention for the public health. *J Med Ethics* 26, 157–9; Coker, R. (2000). The law, human rights, and the detention of individuals with tuberculosis in England and Wales. *J Public Health Med* 22, 263–7. A useful pair of linked contributions to this issue.

9. Department of Health (2007). *Review of Parts II, IV and VI of the Public Health (Control of Disease) Act 1984: Report on Consultation*. London: Department of Health.

10. Some of this legislation has yet to come into force and, at the time of writing, it is unclear how the new coalition government in the UK will develop the legislative agenda in relation to health and social care.

11. [2005] ECHR.

12. The figures show a steady increase in the numbers of Deprivation of Liberty orders: between July and September 2010, there were 2,333 orders, which represented an

increase of 39%; see Lewis, S. (2011). Deprivation of Liberty order use rises. *Health Service Journal*, 13 January 2011.

13. See, for example, Meikle, J. (2011). Court allows journalists into care hearing. *The Guardian*, 28 February 2011; and Gordon, C. (2011). Son 'not harmed by publicity' judge rules. *The Independent*, 2 March 2011.

14. Cutter, W., Greenberg, K., Nicholson, T. R. and Cairns, R. (2011). *Identifying and managing deprivation of liberty in adults in England and Wales. BMJ* **342**, 163–8.

Continuing consent: does the patient still agree?

Introduction

Seeking and obtaining consent is commonly represented as a single act. The patient presents, and the clinician explains what he or she wishes to do and seeks the patient's agreement to implement investigations and treatment. The paperwork is signed, the forms sent off and consent is complete. This routine conceptualization of consent does not capture a significant component of proper consent, namely that it is continuing or ongoing. Merely because someone once agreed to, or indeed refused, an investigation, procedure or treatment, it does not mean that consent endures indefinitely. Yet like the requirement that consent be voluntary, the value of ensuring that consent is continuing is often overlooked in the literature. Where it is discussed in detail, it is most likely to be in the context of research where a participant's ongoing willingness to be part of a trial or study is often built into the protocol and emphasized as part of the process of obtaining ethical approval. This chapter will consider the concept of continuing consent in the context of clinical practice rather than biomedical research, and will discuss some of the issues and challenges that can arise.

Continuing consent and the process of healthcare

As discussions in earlier chapters have stressed, healthcare is increasingly systematized. The majority of patients will have contact with a number of healthcare professionals. The journey through the healthcare system commonly begins in primary care. It may take several visits to a GP practice before referrals are made and those primary care consultations are likely to involve history taking, investigations and some treatment. If a referral is considered to be appropriate, this may happen some time after the patient originally presented and is likely to be at an institution that is new to the patient. When the patient attends for his or her referral appointment, the process of history taking, examinations and investigations resume leading perhaps to surgery, treatment or procedures. Further referrals may follow, sometimes accompanied by requests to participate in teaching, educational activities, service evaluation, audits or research. The patient may encounter many people along the way: GPs, nurses, hospital doctors, phlebotomists, radiographers, physiotherapists, physician assistants, anaesthetists, ward clerks, occupational therapists, auxiliary staff, clinical and non-clinical managers, healthcare students, speech and language therapists, receptionists, secretaries and pharmacists may all contribute to an individual's care. Healthcare is rarely, if ever, a one-off transaction between an individual practitioner and patient. It is almost always a process over a period of time involving many people.

It is not only the range of people involved in healthcare that makes the case for the value and importance of continuing consent. The content of healthcare encompasses multiple decision points and a variety of activities that may not seem, to the patient, to be obviously related or integrated. Consider the scenario below.

Mr Jacobson is a 52-year-old man who attends a Well Man Clinic led by a nurse at his local GP surgery. During the consultation, Mr Jacobson tells the nurse that he has been feeling 'run down' and has lost weight, which he attributes to not being able to eat as much as usual due to 'indigestion'. The nurse tells Mr Jacobson that she would like him to see one of the GPs. A week later, one of the GP partners, Dr Harmer, sees Mr Jacobson. He takes a history and performs a basic examination. He does not find any abnormalities on examination but records Mr Jacobson's symptoms of indigestion and notes his recent weight loss. Dr Harmer prescribes ranitidine for Mr Jacobson's gastric symptoms and asks him to attend the local phlebotomy clinic for blood tests. Mr Jacobson has his prescription dispensed and attends for blood tests. He returns to the GP surgery 10 days later where he sees Dr Harmer's GP Registrar, Dr Mehta. Dr Mehta explains that the blood results are normal and asks about Mr Jacobson's symptoms. Mr Jacobson reports that he is still feeling 'below par' and that his gastric symptoms appear to be worsening rather than improving. Dr Mehta suggests that Mr Jacobson try omeprazole as an alternative to ranitidine and that he be referred for further investigation by a hospital team. Eight weeks later, Mr Jacobson attends an outpatient appointment with Dr Kranzcwyck. Dr Kranzcwyck takes a history and performs a thorough physical examination. He orders blood tests and suggests that an endoscopy and colonoscopy would be useful. Dr Kranzcwyck also queries the use of omeprazole and explains that he would prefer that Mr Jacobson takes lansoprazole which is the 'first-line choice'. A fortnight later, Mr Jacobson receives the bowel preparation kit from the hospital along with instructions for use which he follows. Mr Jacobson attends for his endoscopy and colonoscopy, which are performed by Dr Milson whom Mr Jacobson has not previously met. A couple of weeks later, Mr Jacobson returns to his GP surgery where he is seen by a locum, Dr Hayward. Dr Hayward explains that the endoscopy and colonoscopy did not show anything significant but that the blood results from the hospital show that he has a raised erythrocyte sedimentation rate (ESR) and C-reactive protein (CRP). Mr Jacobson reports new symptoms of increased malaise and a persistent cough. Dr Hayward suggests that Mr Jacobson should return to the hospital for further investigation. Four weeks later, Mr Jacobson is seen in an outpatient clinic by Dr Koromba who explains that she would like to investigate the cause of Mr Jacobson's symptoms and raised ESR/CRP levels.

Mr Jacobson is not experiencing anything particularly unusual in his contacts with the healthcare system: it is a routine account of one person's journey through the NHS. The involvement of multiple practitioners from different specialties offering a range of expertise and skills is often perceived as an advantage of the NHS. Indeed, a few years ago, there was a national NHS recruitment campaign that highlighted the numbers of professionals involved in a single person's healthcare. Yet with the various clinical encounters Mr Jacobson experiences come multiple opportunities for consent to be sought.

It is worth looking beyond the routine to consider the nature of consent that is likely to have been sought and the extent to which that consent was considered to apply to a chain of events. Firstly, Mr Jacobson presents to the practice nurse for a check-up as part of a clinic with a specific remit, namely the Well Man Clinic. It is reasonable to expect that Mr Jacobson has a broad idea of what to expect as part of a visit to such a clinic. The nurse refers Mr Jacobson to a GP in the practice for further discussion of the symptoms he disclosed in his consultation with her. Dr Harmer assumes responsibility for seeking consent for what is to follow. Dr Harmer probably assumes that Mr Jacobson's responses constitute agreement to participate in the consultation and to allow Dr Harmer to take a history and perform an examination. The request that Mr Jacobson attends the phlebotomy clinic and the prescription of ranitidine will probably be explained in more detail to Mr Jacobson. However, it is worth pausing as an aside to consider the nature of the discussion about Mr Jacobson attending the phlebotomy clinic; is it likely to be a conversation that is about the practicalities of having blood taken (e.g. the location and opening hours of the clinic) or a substantive discussion of the reasons for taking blood and the probable tests that will be conducted? By attending the phlebotomy clinic and filling his prescription for ranitidine, Mr Jacobson may be said to be agreeing to these parts of the process of seeking and obtaining treatment.

The next consultation with Dr Mehta is clearly related to the previous contacts with the practice nurse, Dr Harmer, the phlebotomist and the pharmacist. Yet this is a new consultation and it is good practice for Dr Mehta to review what has already happened with Mr Jacobson. Just because Mr Jacobson has already consented to taking one proton pump inhibitor (PPI), does that mean that Dr Mehta's substitution of omeprazole for ranitidine is 'covered' by the original consent? That seems unlikely. Exploring what Mr Jacobson understands about his symptoms, the investigations he has had thus far and the reasons for being prescribed a PPI is essential for Dr Mehta. Some might suggest that, because Mr Jacobson has attended the consultation, he is agreeing to participate in whatever history-taking, examinations, investigations and treatment that Dr Mehta believes to be indicated: what might be described as 'assumed consent on the basis of walking through the door'. It may not surprise readers to learn that such 'consent' is undesirable and unacceptable. There are many reasons why people attend medical appointments. Some come seeking information, others are exploring options or hoping for reassurance, still more may visit a doctor because a third party has nagged them into doing so and a minority even believe that they are obliged to attend in particular circumstances, for example to collect the results of tests, when a referral to secondary care has been made or they are invited to take part in a screening programme. Many people will not have given the reasons for, or implications of, their attendance at a medical appointment a moment's thought; to walk through the door cannot be assumed to be considered, informed or voluntary. Mr Jacobson is relying on Dr Mehta to help him make a more considered, informed and voluntary choice about his healthcare. Dr Mehta must combine the past and present accounts of Mr Jacobson's experience as part of the consent process: omeprazole is preferred to ranitidine and a referral is indicated because Mr Jacobson's experience has changed and his symptoms have worsened – it is a new stage in the clinical journey and seeking consent marks that new stage.

When Mr Jacobson attends his outpatient appointment, once again consent is to be sought anew. Dr Kranzcwyck is meeting Mr Jacobson for the first time and, just as he is likely to take a history and perform examinations for himself rather than rely solely on the findings of his GP colleagues, so too should Dr Kranzcwyck seek and obtain consent for himself. The content of the consultation is likely to cover some familiar territory but it will also introduce new elements such as the colonoscopy and endoscopy, further blood tests and the change from omeprazole to lansoprazole. At this point in his journey, Mr Jacobson is likely to have questions, and those questions reflect the ongoing nature of modern healthcare. For example, whilst Dr Kranzcwyck is meeting and prescribing for Mr Jacobson for the first time, his medication has been changed three times in a relatively short period of time and he has had a number of blood tests.

The arrival in the post of the bowel preparation kit and written instructions is both familiar and fascinating. At this point, human interaction is replaced by a leaflet. It suggests that it is the provision of information that is privileged[1] and considered to be central with no attention given to the other three elements of consent, namely capacity, voluntariness and its continuing nature. When Dr Milson meets Mr Jacobson for the first time, it is to do two invasive procedures. Dr Milson may assume that consent has largely been sought via prior conversations with clinicians and the provision of information about the endoscopy and colonoscopy that was sent in the post. However, by so doing, Dr Milson too would be reducing consent to the exchange of information and disregarding the other elements of consent. Mr Jacobson's experiences, perceptions, priorities and concerns may have changed, perhaps considerably. Mr Jacobson may have a particular response to the specific investigations that Dr Milson is planning to carry out. It may be clear to Dr Milson that the proposed investigations are part of the overall clinical picture but far from obvious to Mr Jacobson. All of these significant and unspoken elements will be overlooked unless Dr Milson attends to the ongoing nature of consent. It is Dr Milson's role to locate the encounter in the bigger clinical context and to establish how Mr Jacobson feels about the investigations and their possible consequences at the time they meet each other. Consent must be alert to context and what has gone before, but it should not be historical.

An endoscopy and colonoscopy are likely to be, to use a well-worn clinical adjective, 'uncomfortable' for Mr Jacobson. There is much in medicine that creates discomfort and even pain. The ethical rationale is, of course, that it is likely to lead to an outcome that is in the patient's best interests. Most people understand that the temporary experience of an uncomfortable investigation or procedure is justifiable because of the anticipation of positive long-term effects on health. However, to return to the subject of this chapter – consent as a continuing process – what are the potential implications of this daily experience of clinicians causing temporary discomfort for longer-term gain? If Dr Milson begins the endoscopy and Mr Jacobson becomes distressed, is unable to swallow the tube and resists the endoscope, does that mean that he is withdrawing his consent? If Dr Milson continues to try to make Mr Jacobson swallow the tube even in the face of physical and verbal resistance, is Dr Milson disregarding the ongoing nature of consent?

Perhaps the first stage in considering when a patient's natural reluctance and instinctive resistance to a painful procedure compromises the continuing nature of consent is to ensure that honest information about what might ensue as part of the procedure should always encompass the likely level of discomfort or pain. If Dr Milson explains to Mr Jacobson that the degree of discomfort is variable and that some patients find it such that they seek to withdraw consent, there can be an open discussion of the value of sedation (including noting that it can be unpredictably effective or, sometimes, ineffective), Mr Jacobson's priorities and concerns, Dr Milson's clinical preferences and the likely consequences of a refusal of consent for Mr Jacobson's future healthcare. If there are any circumstances in which Dr Milson would proceed even in the face of Mr Jacobson's withdrawal of consent, these should be explained and discussed. Indeed, some NHS Trusts have recognized that the ongoing nature and withdrawal of consent when performing endoscopies is a significant issue in clinical practice, and specific guidelines have been developed to cover the situation.[2] Just as Mr Jacobson's permission should be informed, so too should his refusal during the procedure. It may be that there are particular reasons why the endoscopy or colonoscopy becomes more painful or uncomfortable at times. Mr Jacobson should understand the level of analgesia available to him and how to indicate that he would like more. There might be an agreement to ensure that a third party, perhaps an endoscopy nurse, advocates Mr Jacobson and focuses solely on his needs, interests and wishes while ensuring that he continues to be informed about the progress of the procedures. Mr Jacobson should understand what would happen if the procedures were stopped and how his symptoms could be managed and/or further investigated. This is the business of a skilled consultation prior to the procedures and effective communication by an experienced clinician throughout – it is an ethical responsibility far beyond that which can be met by a patient information leaflet and instructions enclosed with a bowel preparation kit that arrive in the post.

Refusal of consent may not mean an immediate end to the procedures. It is possible that Mr Jacobson needs to pause. It may be sufficient for Dr Milson to take a moment to explain what is happening and to give Mr Jacobson an opportunity to share how he is feeling. To construct the dilemma as a binary battle where either Dr Milson continues irrespective of Mr Jacobson's wishes and completes without delay or Mr Jacobson calls time on the investigations and everything stops immediately is unhelpful. The continuing nature of consent is not a burden but an opportunity. It acknowledges that healthcare is complex and not linear. It allows, even demands, that clinicians and their patients take the time to share their perspectives and work together towards an acceptable process and outcome. It is not an impediment to swift and efficient healthcare but a conduit for trust, respect and an effective therapeutic relationship.

As Mr Jacobson's journey through the NHS continues, his results are sent to his GP surgery where he is seen by a sixth healthcare professional, Dr Hayward. Dr Hayward's task is to review the clinical progress to date, discuss the results from the endoscopy, colonoscopy and blood tests with Mr Jacobson and to explore his new symptoms of a persistent cough and increased malaise. It may appear as though Dr Hayward's role is that of information provider and interpreter of secondary care results. Some may think that there is little in the way of seeking or obtaining consent required of Dr Hayward, but that would be a mistake. Dr Hayward is, at the time of the consultation, responsible for maintaining the continuity of the process. It is his role to ensure that Mr Jacobson not only understands the potential significance of the results from the hospital but that he is able to make a choice about how to proceed from here. Dr Hayward may be doing nothing in the way of examination, investigation, diagnosis or treatment, but he is vital in ensuring that Mr Jacobson is able to make ongoing choices about how his health is managed. It is only by Dr Hayward explaining the results, contextualizing the potential meanings of those results, exploring the options for future care and listening to

Mr Jacobson's views, concerns and priorities that consent to timely and appropriate follow-up can exist. Dr Hayward is the linchpin in the ongoing business of consent and he is crucial to Mr Jacobson's well-being. It is a consultation that may appear to be relatively simple from a clinical point of view, but from an ethical perspective, it is fundamental.

Mr Jacobson's case ends with his referral from Dr Hayward to Dr Koromba (the seventh professional he has encountered), who, we are told, wishes to conduct her own investigations. Constraints of space and a wish to avoid labouring the point mean that we leave Mr Jacobson there and do not know anything more about his journey through the NHS. What the discussion of Mr Jacobson's experience has shown is that clinicians inevitably encounter patients at all stages of their progress through the monolithic and systemic maze of healthcare. Each clinician brings specific expertise to the care of a patient and that expertise shapes not only the clinical contribution but the ways in which consent is sought and obtained. It is only by reflecting both on what has gone before and on what may follow that it is possible for consent to be meaningfully ongoing. It is a balancing act that requires clinicians to be aware of what has preceded as well as what may ensue, while also ensuring that they seek proper consent for their part in the patient's care. One should neither rely solely and exclusively on, nor disregard entirely, the consent sought by others. Healthcare is a process, and so too is seeking and obtaining consent. An awareness of that process and where one sits within it is vital to ensuring that consent is ongoing and meaningful.

Continuity of consent and changes in identity

Changes in identity have significant implications for the ongoing nature of consent. Changes in identity may affect both patient and clinician and each version is discussed in this section.

Changing clinicians

An important element of Mr Jacobson's case was the number of different clinicians he encountered. However, those changes in identity were to be expected and were inevitable in a healthcare system where primary care acts as a gate to secondary care in which specialist services are increasingly delineated. Most patients understand that the doctor that they will see when they visit the outpatient clinic will not be the GP who referred them and that future introductions will be made should they be referred subsequently to another department or become an inpatient. A different issue may arise when the identity of a doctor changes within a clinical team, perhaps especially if there is also a change in the experience or status of the doctor. Consider the scenario below.

Mr Marcus Bayton is a 51-year-old man. He has type II diabetes, hypertension and his body mass index is 46. Mr Bayton was referred by his GP to discuss his possible suitability for bariatric surgery. Mr Bayton was initially reluctant but eventually attended the outpatient clinic of Mr Krishna, who is a leading figure in the field of bariatric surgery and has an international reputation. Mr Bayton liked Mr Krishna and agreed to meet the rest of his team, including a dietician, an endocrinologist, a psychiatrist, an anaesthetist and a specialist nurse. Eventually, Mr Bayton went on the waiting list for surgery. Seven months later, Mr Bayton received a date for his operation. When he arrived at the hospital, Mr Bayton was surprised to be seen by Mr Papadakis, who introduced himself as Mr Krishna's colleague. Mr Bayton asked why Mr Krishna was unavailable to meet him. Mr Papadakis explained that he had left to work at a hospital in the USA. On questioning by Mr Bayton, Mr Papadakis explained that he was a specialist trainee who was 'very close' to having his own consultant job and he reassured Mr Bayton that he had worked a great deal with Mr Krishna before he left the hospital for his new position.

The experience of Mr Bayton is common in the NHS. Clinicians, especially those in training, frequently move to new roles in different locations. The composition of most clinical teams is constantly changing and is inevitably dynamic. Even when members of staff remain in post for a long time, shift patterns, personal circumstances, annual leave and changes in responsibilities mean that it is impossible to guarantee who an individual patient will see. Healthcare works on the basis that members of staff are competent to fulfil a particular role in a team that contains a range of expertise and experience. Clinicians function according to role and level of training. The mysteries of the therapeutic relationship are such that for many, both staff and patients, some clinicians are more appealing than others. Most readers will be able to call to mind quickly those colleagues with whom one both prefers to work and would prefer to be a patient. For patients like Mr Bayton who are apprehensive, mistrustful and wary, the attachment to an individual clinician – in this case, Mr Krishna – can be significant. From the limited information in the vignette, it seems that Mr Bayton has struggled to access clinical treatment and that his relationship with a particular surgeon was a significant part of him agreeing to treatment. It is impossible to quantify the influence that Mr Krishna, as an individual surgeon, had on Mr Bayton, but it is noteworthy both that Mr Bayton is said to have liked Mr Krishna sufficiently to meet the rest of the team and that Mr Krishna has an international reputation. It seems improbable that the combined effect of interpersonal connection between Mr Bayton and Mr Krishna and the outstanding professional status of the latter did not influence Mr Bayton considerably.

What then is the likely effect of Mr Papadakis on the continuing nature of consent? As far as the healthcare system goes, it is negligible: team members change regularly and as long as there are people with the relevant qualifications and experience working at the required level with appropriate supervision and support, the standard of care remains constant. Individual patients in the NHS are not able to request treatment by a specific clinician. Even with the recent emphasis on patient choice, via initiatives such as 'Choose and Book',[3] the scope of individual preference has been limited to hospital location and appointment dates and times. It is only in the private sector that patients are able to make choices about individual clinicians. Yet unsurprisingly, the identity of the clinician is important to the vast majority of patients. It is well documented that complaints and litigation are commonly based on what might be called failures of the interpersonal or clinical relationships that have gone awry. Healthcare is an inherently human endeavour in which strong interpersonal relationships form the foundation for effective clinical practice.

The task then for Mr Papadakis is to acknowledge the surprise and perhaps concern that Mr Krishna's departure is likely to have caused Mr Bayton. Empathy and imagination on the part of Mr Papadakis will quickly ensure that he realizes that Mr Bayton is a vulnerable patient who is naturally apprehensive of the change of personnel, especially given his initial reluctance to seek treatment and the stigma that such patients often feel. Taking the time to talk to Mr Bayton and to acknowledge his reservations and concerns will be time well spent. It may be tempting for Mr Papadakis to emphasize that he is more than amply qualified to conduct surgery on Mr Bayton and that he has considerable professional expertise and experience. However natural it may be to stress accomplishment and professional status, to do so risks appearing to disregard the patient's concerns and might even seem as defensive. Mr Bayton is likely to know rationally that Mr Papadakis is sufficiently skilled to operate and that there is appropriate senior support available. It is not a matter of rationality, however, but emotion. Mr Bayton is scared, worried and concerned that the surgeon whom he learned to trust and in whom he cautiously placed his faith has been replaced by a stranger immediately before a life-changing operation. It is only by acknowledging and responding to these feelings that Mr Papadakis is likely to ensure that the consent Mr Bayton initially gave to Mr Krishna will continue to enable Mr Papadakis to perform the operation.

In practical terms, when seeking consent from a patient where the identity of the clinician has changed, there may be specific considerations when sharing information. For example, Mr Bayton may wish to know about the specific surgical experience and outcomes of operations performed by Mr Papadakis. Mr Bayton may ask whether Mr Papadakis is going to be supervised as he is still awaiting a consultant's post and if so, whether that supervision is in the form of senior advice on the end of a telephone or someone who is physically present in theatre. Mr Papadakis will wish to review the findings of clinicians to date and consider whether there is any information missing or that he would like to confirm. The wider membership of the multidisciplinary team whom

Mr Bayton has met might be helpful in facilitating the relationship between the new surgeon and patient. If Mr Bayton sees that Mr Papadakis both respects and is respected by Mr Krishna's old colleagues, he is likely to find it easier to build a relationship with Mr Papadakis.

What would the position be if Mr Bayton were ultimately to insist that he wished only to have surgery performed by a surgeon with directly equivalent experience and status to Mr Krishna? Or even, in a somewhat unlikely turn of events, if Mr Bayton were to demand that Mr Krishna himself be required to return to perform the operation as originally planned? In short, Mr Bayton would be disappointed. Just as patients are not entitled to demand particular treatment, they are not able to request that a particular doctor or surgeon provides care. Even in general practice, patients are commonly registered with a GP practice rather than an individual GP. In the ever-decreasing GP surgeries where individual doctors do have named patient lists, there will be provision for care to be shared with other doctors when necessary. It is simply not possible within the NHS to accommodate preferences for individual clinicians. That said, by acknowledging the effect of a different clinician on trust and consent, it is likely that many would conclude that there is moral value in continuity of care. It is not merely that it is a 'nice' way to practise medicine or that patients may prefer continuity, but that such continuity positively enhances the enactment of meaningful consent.

Changing patients

It is not just clinicians whose identities can change and affect consent. Patients too may experience fundamental shifts in identity, albeit of a more philosophical kind. In a sense, any experience of illness and disease is identity-changing. The shift from health to impairment, from freedom to the burden of symptoms, from independence to dependence and from strength to vulnerability can be transformative. There is an expansive literature on the nature of illness and becoming a patient, which leaves the reader in little doubt that, whilst the changes that occur when one is ill may not be wholly negative, they are substantive and far-reaching. The concept of the 'pre-morbid' personality[4] is fascinating and acknowledges, in a particularly clinical way, that to become ill is to alter fundamentally. Perhaps the best way to capture the encompassing effects of illness on oneself is in the words of Dr Jonathan Miller who, writing in his book *The Body in Question* said that '*illness is not something a person has; it's another way of being*'.[5]

For the purposes of consent, the state of illness itself can impair or change the standard currency of sharing information and seeking permission. Symptoms may compromise capacity or lead to a preoccupation with particular pieces of information. Dependence on others may render the voluntariness of consent questionable. However, for the purposes of this chapter on the continuing nature of consent, it is worth taking a moment to consider how the effects of illness and being a patient may themselves inform the process of seeking and obtaining consent. Consider the scenario below.

Mrs Lucas, aged 34, is a solicitor who is married and has one child. She was referred to her local hospital by her GP after she found a lump in her breast. Mrs Lucas had never had any previous health problems and she had only encountered doctors for travel injections, minor infections and routine antenatal care. Mrs Lucas was seen swiftly at the hospital and, following fine needle aspiration, was diagnosed with early-stage breast cancer. She was given the choice of a lumpectomy or a mastectomy because the cancer was believed to be small and contained. Mrs Lucas chose to have a lumpectomy. Surgery was followed by a discussion about whether Mrs Lucas wished to have radiation therapy. She declined and had hormone therapy alone. Six years later, Mrs Lucas found another lump. She had a double mastectomy and several lymph nodes were removed. After surgery, she had two cycles of chemotherapy. Eighteen months later, Mrs Lucas presented to her GP with cough, malaise and breathlessness. She was seen by the oncology team within a week. The breast cancer had spread to the lungs and the options were discussed with Mrs Lucas. Her doctors explained that the active treatment options were unfortunately limited but that there were several ways in which good symptomatic control could be achieved. The idea of being seen by the palliative care team was also introduced. Mrs Lucas eventually died five months later, aged 43, in a hospice.

Mrs Lucas is undoubtedly going to be irrevocably changed by her journey from an independent working mother to a dying woman. At each stage, Mrs Lucas is likely to have had different priorities, specific questions, unspoken fears, politely reframed concerns and shifting emotions. The woman who gave consent for the lumpectomy was not the same as the woman who made the final decision to be transferred to the hospice. In purely legal terms, those changes matter little unless they affect Mrs Lucas's capacity, in which case the panoply of provisions intended to support decision-making come into play. However, from an ethical perspective and specifically in relation to the continuing nature of consent, the dynamic, complex and sometimes contradictory feelings, experiences, impulses and motivations that Mrs Lucas is likely to have had inevitably inform her choices and relationship with the healthcare professionals offering her care. It is impossible to see the continuing nature of consent as not requiring clinicians to be alert and responsive to the changing identities of their patients. To do otherwise would be to reduce patients to stages of disease, treatment protocols and management pathways. To obtain consent is to engage with the individual person. Just as consent must be seen as continuing in its clinical context with reference to what has gone before and its effects on the present, so too must consent be seen as continuing in the personal context with reference to what this patient has experienced and felt before and its effects on the present. What is more, whilst illness changes people, so too do people change illness. There is no single experience or neatly categorized narrative for how individuals bear and respond to particular diseases or diagnoses. To understand consent as a continuing and ongoing process is to understand that it is imbued with shifting identities, complex contextualized emotion and idiosyncratic perceptions: ongoing consent is personal and personalized, and changeable and changing.

Where patients change in a way that leads to significant behavioural change or alters relationships, the concept of identity is also relevant. Many clinicians will have heard from families of those with dementia that the patient is 'no longer himself'. Encapsulated in that everyday phrase is an idea that has occupied philosophers, scientists and artists alike for centuries: what is the essence of a human being? What is it that makes us who we are? And, when illness so significantly transforms identity, what are the implications of those changes for choices and decision-making in healthcare? Consider the scenario below.

> Mr Leonard is 79 years old. He has recently been moved to a residential nursing home because his dementia has become more severe and his partner is no longer able to cope with Mr Leonard at home. One day, Mr Leonard's partner visits him in the residential home. She is horrified to find that Mr Leonard is tucking in with gusto to a beef casserole. She explains to the staff that Mr Leonard is a committed vegetarian who has not eaten meat for over 60 years since he was a teenager. A member of staff explains that Mr Leonard appears to enjoy eating meat a great deal; in fact, he becomes distressed and agitated when meat is not on the menu.

The natural tendency, particularly when thinking about consent, is to frame the issues with reference to autonomy and self-determination. The fact that consent is an ongoing process is therefore framed as providing multiple opportunities for self-determination. Yet embedded in the notion of self-determination are moral assumptions about personhood, identity and relationships. Respect for autonomy too often depends on a shared definition of personhood that is characterized by the ability to remember and to comprehend.[6] In cases such as that of Mr Leonard, constancy of identity and continuity of narrative appear to be inapplicable: he is no longer able to identify himself as a non-meat eater. His identity as a vegetarian is located entirely in the memory of others, such as his partner. However, even with his cognitive impairment, Mr Leonard is able to convey preference about his food (and presumably many other aspects of his daily life). In a thought-provoking analysis of cognitive impairment and its effects on identity and choice, Stephen Post[7] argues for moral recognition of what he calls people's 'essential humanity', whatever cognitive decline may have occurred. In the case of Mr Leonard, such essential humanity might include the freedom to express a preference about the food that he eats. He may no longer be capable of making a political or values-based decision about his diet, but he is able to convey what he wants to eat and when he wants to eat it. Mr Leonard may sometimes not meet the criteria required for a capacitous decision in complex circumstances, but he does retain the ability to express a preference about food. It may be a choice that reflects a change in identity or even a choice that is seen by some as pathological in origin, but nonetheless Mr Leonard is able to convey his own wishes. His past may be lost and his future uncertain, but in the present and on one fundamental matter, Mr Leonard is able to choose as well as anyone. His changed identity has altered the content of his decision-making about food, but it has not altered his ability to make those decisions. In such situations, the value of consent as an ongoing and dynamic process is vitally important. By conveying preferences, Mr Leonard not only has the meals he prefers but is afforded respect and moral status.

Continuing consent: concluding thoughts

This chapter has looked at one of the least discussed elements of consent: the notion of consent as an ongoing or continuing process. The variables that can compromise or contribute to consent being truly continuing include the complex systemic structures within which healthcare is delivered, changes in the membership of clinical teams, the transformative effect of illness on people and the particular effects of cognitive impairment on notions of personhood and identity. The common theme that recurs in the discussion of each of those factors is continuity of care and its moral value. Increasingly, continuity of care is difficult to achieve in the NHS, yet it is undoubtedly a powerful tool in ensuring that meaningful, ongoing consent is achieved. In the absence of systemic support for continuity of care, all clinicians have to reflect on how they fit into both the system of healthcare provision and their patients' lives. We hope that this chapter has helped in that task.

Endnotes

1. It also, of course, privileges literacy and language, but this is beyond the remit of this chapter.

2. See, for example, Royal United Hospital Bath NHS Trust (2007). *Withdrawal of Consent for an Endoscopic Procedure.* Available at: http://www.ruh.nhs.uk/about/policies/docu ments/clinical_policies/local/412_Withdrawal_of_consent_for_an_endoscopic_proced ure.pdf.

3. http://www.chooseandbook.nhs.uk

4. It is also fascinating and noteworthy that the majority of work exploring the notion of 'pre-morbid personality' is to be found in studies concerned with neurological and psychiatric impairment, such as research conducted with those who have dementia or schizophrenia when the question of the effects of sickness on identity is equally applicable to the experience of physical illness.

5. Miller, J. (1979). *The Body in Question*. New York: Random House.

6. Kitwood, T. (1997) *Dementia Reconsidered. The Person Comes First*. Buckingham: Open University Press.

7. Post, S. G. (2006). Respectare: Moral Respect for the Lives of the Deeply Forgetful. In J. C. Hughes, S. J. Louw and S. R. Sabat, eds., *Dementia: Mind, Meaning and the Person*. Oxford: Oxford University Press.

Chapter

6

Concluding thoughts on consent

The opportunity to write is always an opportunity to learn. As a mixed authorial team, we have benefited from sharing our perspectives on, and experiences of, consent. This sort of productive and stimulating cross-disciplinary learning might have been anticipated. What was perhaps less predictable is the effect of revisiting, reviewing and reconsidering that most fundamental of concepts: consent. Readers will be reassured to know that the terrain was, we believed, familiar to and well trodden by us when we commenced this book.

We had reason to be confident: we knew the key cases, professional guidance and policy documents on consent thoroughly and we had spent many hours considering the conceptual ways in which the ethics literature has discussed autonomy, self-determination and the moral value of consent. The clinical enactment of consent in daily medical practice was also familiar, and we had views from both primary and secondary care in our team. Yet our confidence was tempered with wariness. The consequence of knowing the literature well and having a breadth of clinical experience was that we understood that there is a vast array of resources for those seeking guidance on consent. What was it that we could bring to the subject that was novel and informative?

Initially, the idea to structure the book by breaking down consent into its constituent parts was largely a functional decision. It was a neat way to discuss the different elements of consent that mirrored the law and professional guidance while allowing a multifaceted ethical discussion that was integrated and relevant. It also had a pragmatic purpose in that such organization allowed a fair distribution of labour in this multi-authored book and provided an opportunity for us to explore particular areas of interest. As we began to write, however, it quickly became clear that, by looking again at the composite elements of consent and revisiting what had initially seemed so familiar, we were doing something unexpected that took us beyond repackaging the existing body of work on consent with some novel clinical examples.

Firstly, we discovered an imbalance in the ways in which consent is presented. A great deal of attention has been afforded to capacity and the provision of information, but relatively little attention had been paid to the importance of voluntariness and the requirement that consent be an ongoing or continuing process. The work that existed in relation to voluntariness and the continuing nature of consent was largely focused on biomedical research and consent in the context of trials. This is a curious finding. Consent is, of course, highly regulated and normatively defined in relation to research as a result of the oversight of research ethics committees and procedures for research governance. This is a book about clinical practice and the specific requirements of consent for research were outwith the remit of this text, but it is noteworthy that the standards for consent in relation to research are both more formalized and more even in the attention afforded to all its constituent parts prompting the question: why? Voluntariness and an ongoing commitment are as important in clinical practice as in biomedical research. We hope that the discussion in Chapters 4 and 5 of this book go some way to redressing the balance and highlight the rather neglected value of attending to voluntariness and consent as a continuing process in clinical practice.

The second discovery from writing this book in this way and at this time concerned the translation of the existing work on consent to daily clinical work, be it in primary or secondary care. The excellent materials that exist already on the subject of consent cover the full range from short 'how to' guides to densely argued philosophical monographs, with every shade of publication in between. Yet our clinical experience told us that there were routine situations encountered by doctors and patients every day that were not captured within the available literature. The shades of grey, the ambiguities and the overlooked nuances of practice came to the fore as we realized that even those who spend a lot of time studying and writing about ethics struggle with the translation of that learning to clinical practice. All of the scenarios in this book are (anonymized and composite) examples from clinical practice of situations where, over the years, we have wondered about seeking and obtaining consent in a way that is ethically robust and located in the generally accepted principles of valid consent. The clinical scenarios we have chosen are designed to make visible the invisible questions and assumptions that imbue medicine and healthcare on a daily basis. We have done so not with the aim of making life even more difficult for busy clinicians but with the aim of inviting the reader to reflect on his or her practice and perhaps to prompt discussion within teams or even with patients. The discussions that follow each scenario are intended to act as triggers for thought and debate, not as normative rules or immutable principles to follow slavishly. The amount of discretion each clinician has when he or she seeks and obtains consent is considerable and that became clearer the more we wrote and talked about this book.

The third discovery was about the nature of a 'primer'. We had accepted the brief from the publisher with a vague idea of what this title might offer that was unique and of value. We believed that there was a gap for a book that drew on the conceptual framework of consent but was firmly focused on clinical practice. We felt that many of our clinical colleagues are well versed in the building blocks of consent, which are examined in medical school, work-based assessments and membership examinations. Another title that reiterated the importance of consent and summarized the key issues was not required. However, a title that allowed clinicians to review the 'basics' while thinking about the implications in a determinedly clinical context and developing a deeper understanding of consent was an attractive goal. A book that could be accurately described as a 'primer' was an exciting prospect. Whilst there is a standard definition of the 'primer' as a text that covers the basic elements of a subject, we increasingly had the verb 'to prime' in mind as we wrote and discussed this book. We felt it was a title that we hoped would prepare and develop clinicians personally and professionally. The preparation and development was squarely aimed at enhancing clinical practice, rather than producing nascent ethicists. The aim was to take the basics of consent and present them in a novel, stimulating and thought-provoking way, giving each of the four elements of consent equal and special attention with multiple clinical examples to illustrate the points.

We end the book with some recommendations from the general literature, that is to say the non-clinical literature, as a means of enhancing the understanding of this material more completely. Notes have been used throughout as an optional means of the reader diving a little deeper into these issues via other academic writings. The last part of this chapter will offer contributions from great writers and interpreters who have considered the nature of health, disease, encounters with medicine and the issues of consent in their own individual ways and who, we believe, have something to offer. In a book that emphasizes the inherent humanity that is negotiated in seeking and obtaining consent, some of the richest resources are, perhaps inevitably, to be found in the humanities. In our teaching and personal reflection we have found these works from literature, theatre and film to be of value. Consider it as a virtual book club or an invitation to the theatre or cinema.

The desire to break something down to understand its workings better is an age-old impulse. Children and adults alike relish the chance to dissect, disassemble and deconstruct. We hope that impulse applies to consent. By breaking it down and looking at its constituent parts, we have seen consent in new and exciting ways. We hope that the same can be said of our readers.

The reading room

Fiction

Zola, E. (1893). *Doctor Pascal*. Oxford: Oxford University Press.
Alcott, L. M. (1960). *Hospital Sketches*. Cambridge, MA: Harvard University Press.
Green, H. (1967). *I Never Promised You a Rose Garden*. London: Pan Books.
Murdoch, I. (1968). *The Nice and the Good*. New York: Viking.
Solzhenitsyn, (1971). A. *Cancer Ward*. London: Penguin.

Burgess. A. (1972). *The Doctor is Sick*. London: Penguin.

Burgess, A. (1972). *A Clockwork Orange*. London: Penguin.

Murdoch, I. (1976). *The Sacred and Profane Love Machine*. London: Penguin.

Chekhov, A. (1984). The Doctor's Visit. In *The Lady with the Dog and Other Stories*. New York: Ecco.

Eliot, G. (1986). *Middlemarch*. Oxford: Clarendon Press.

Byatt, A. S. (1994). *The Matisse Stories*. London: Vintage.

Ignatieff, M. (1994). *Scar Tissue*. London: Vintage.

Bulgakov, M. (1995). *A Country Doctor's Notebook*. London: Harvill Press.

Saramago, J. (1997). *Blindness*. London: Vintage.

Pears, I. (1998). *An Instance of the Fingerpost*. London: Vintage.

Selzer, R. (1999). *Doctor Stories*. New York: Picador.

Wharton, E. (2000). *The Fruit of the Tree*. Evanston, IL: Northwestern University Press.

Klass, P. (2001). *Love and Modern Medicine*. Boston, MA: Houghton Mifflin.

Beattie, A. (2002). *The Doctor's House*. New York: Scribner.

Hyland, M. J. (2004). *How the Light Gets In*. Edinburgh: Cannongate.

Kafka, F. (2004). *Metamorphosis*. New York: Crown Publications.

Tolstoy, L. (2004). *Death of Ivan Ilyich and Other Stories (Wordsworth Classics)*. Hertfordshire, UK: Wordsworth Editions Ltd.

Coetzee, J. M. (2006). *Slow Man*. London: Vintage.

McEwan, I. (2006). *Saturday*. London: Vintage.

Lewycka, M. (2006). *A Short History of Tractors in Ukrainian*. London: Penguin.

Vickers, S. (2006). *The Other Side of You*. London: Fourth Estate.

Brooks, G. (2008). *Year of Wonders*. London: Harper Perennial.

Verghese, A. (2009). *Cutting for Stone*. London: Vintage.

Shriver, L. (2011). *So Much for That*. Canada: Harper Collins.

Non-fiction

Gilman, C. P. (1973). *The Yellow Wallpaper*. City University, New York: The Feminist Press. (This is a difficult title to categorize; it is most usually described as part autobiography and part fiction.)

Cooke, A. (1986). *The Patient Has the Floor*. London: The Bodley Head.

Broyard, A. (1993). *Intoxicated By My Illness*. New York: Fawcett.

Redfield-Jamison, K. (1995). *An Unquiet Mind*. New York: Vintage.

Bauby, D.-J. (1998). *The Diving Bell and the Butterfly*. London: Fourth Estate.

Fadiman, A. (1998). *The Spirit Catches You and Then You Fall Down: A Hmong Child, Her American Doctors and the Collision of Two Cultures*. New York: Farrar, Straus & Giroux.

Picardie, R. (1998). *Before I Say Goodbye*. London: Penguin.

Verghese, A. (1998). *The Tennis Partner*. New York: Harper Collins.

Diamond, J. (1999). *C: Because Cowards Get Cancer Too*. London: Vermillion.

Slater, L. (2000). *Spasm: A Memoir with Lies*. London: Methuen Publishing Ltd.

Sanderson, M. (2002). *Wrong Rooms: A Memoir*. London: Scribner.

Woolf, V. (2002). *On Being Ill*. Ashfield, MA: Consortium.

Gawande, A. (2003). *Complications: A Surgeon's Notes on an Imperfect Science*. New York: Picador.

Haddon, M. (2003). *The Curious Incident of the Dog in the Night-time*. New York: Random House.

Mardell, D. (2005). *Danny's Challenge: Learning to Love My Son*. London: Short Books Ltd.

Allen, S. (2007). *Wish I Could Be There: Notes from a Phobic Life*. New York: Viking.

Cavel, H. (2008). *Illness (Art of Living)*. Durham: Acumen Publishing.

Steinberg, J. (2008). *Three Letter Plague*. London: Vintage.

Vernon, M. (2008). *Wellbeing (Art of Living)*. Durham: Acumen Publishing.

Sontag, S. (2009). *Illness as Metaphor and AIDS and its Metaphors*. London: Penguin Classics.

Skloot, R. (2010). *The Immortal Life of Henrietta Lacks*. New York: Random House.

Weston, G. (2010). *Direct Red: A Surgeon's Story*. London: Vintage.

Poetry

Auden, W. H. (1971). Letter to a Wound and Surgical Ward. In *The Selected Poetry of W. H. Auden*. London: Vintage.

Bishop, E. (1983). *The Complete Poems 1927–1979*. New York: Farrar, Straus & Giroux.

Gunn, T. (1992). *The Man with Night Sweats*. New York: Farrar, Straus & Giroux.

Mueller, L. (1996). Monet Refuses the Operation. In *Alive Together: New and Selected Poems*. Eunice, LA: Louisiana State University Press.

Coulehan, J. (2002). *Medicine Stone*. Santa Barbara, CA: Fithian Press.

Fanthorpe, U. A. (2010). *New and Collected Poems*. London: Enitharmon Press.

The theatre

Euripides (431 BC). *Medea*.

Romains, J. (1923). *Dr Knock, or the Triumph of Medicine*.

Marlowe, C. (1588). *Dr Faustus*.

Shakespeare, W. (1605). *King Lear*.

Jonson, B. (1610). *The Alchemist*.

De La Barca, P. C. (1635). *Life is a Dream*.

Moliere (1666). *The Misanthrope*.

Moliere (1673). *The Hypochondriac*.

Goethe, J. W. (1808, 1832). *Faust (Parts 1 & 2)*.

Turgenev, I. (1855). *A Month in the Country*.

Ibsen, H. (1881). *Ghosts*.

Chekhov, A. (1897). *Uncle Vanya*.

Schnitzler, A. (1900). *La Ronde*.

Strindberg, A. (1888). *Miss Julie*.

Bridie, J. (1937). *The Anatomist*.

O' Neill, E. (1931). *Mourning Becomes Electra*.

Brecht, B. (1942). *Mother Courage and Her Children*.

Williams, T. (1944). *The Glass Menagerie*.

Lamont Stewart, E. (1947). *Men Should Weep*.

Stein, G. (1949). *Doctor Faustus Lights the Lights*.

Miller, A. (1953). *The Crucible*.

Osborne, J. (1964). *Inadmissible Evidence*.

Nichols, P. (1967). *A Day in the Death of Joe Egg*.

Beckett, S. (1969). *Breath*.

Erdman, N. (1969). *The Suicide*.

Shaffer, P. (1973). *Equus*.

Pinter, H. (1975). *No Man's Land*.

Shepard, S. (1978). *Buried Child*.

Medoff, M. (1979). *Children of a Lesser God*.

Poliakoff, S. (1984). *Breaking the Silence*.

Dorfman, A. (1990). *Death and the Maiden*.

Mamet, D. (1992). *Oleanna*.

Stoppard, T. (1993). *Arcadia*.

McPherson, C. (1997). *The Weir*.

Frayn, M. (1998). *Copenhagen*.

Auburn, D. (2000). *Proof*.

Penhall, J. (2000). *Blue/Orange*.

Churchill, C. (2002). *A Number*.

Gordon, M. & and Broks, P. (2005). *On Ego*.

Yorkey, B. & and Kitt, T. (2008). *Next to Normal*.

Gordon, M. (2008). *On Emotion*.

Gordon, M. (2010). *Bea*.

Raine, N. (2010). *Tribes*.

Rebellato, D. (2010). *Chekhov in Hell*.

Eldridge, D. (2011). *Knot of the Heart*.

Raine, N. (2011). *Tiger Country*.

The picture house

The Citadel (1938).

A Matter of Life and Death (1946).

The Drunken Angel (1948).

Diary of a Country Priest (1951).

People Will Talk (1951).

Wild Strawberries (1957).

Suddenly Last Summer (1959).

Red Beard (1965).

The Hospital (1971).

One Flew over the Cuckoo's Nest (1975).

Elephant Man (1980).

Ordinary People (1980).

My Left Foot (1989).

City of Joy (1992).

Cancer: A Personal Journey. Notes from the Edge … (1997).

Girl Interrupted (1999).
Kadosh (1999).
A Song for Martin (2001).
Iris (2001).
Wit (2001).
Talk to her (2002).
Eulogy (2004).
The Sea Inside (2004).
Smile (2005).
4 Months, 3 Weeks, 2 Days (2007).
I've Loved You So Long (2008).
Rachel Getting Married (2008).
Boy Interrupted (2009).
Bright Star (2009).
Sons of Lwala (2009).
Ward 6 (2009).
Black Swan (2010).
Never Let Me Go (2010).
Third Star (2011).

Index

3